Motivational Units For Spring

End-of-the-year units and activities to "bridge" home and school, parents and teacher, spring and summer, work and play.

Written and Illustrated by
Susanne Glover and Georgeann Grewe

Cover by Janet Skiles

Copyright © Good Apple, Inc., 1990

ISBN No. 0-86653-524-1

Printing No. 98765432

Good Apple, Inc.
1204 Buchanan, Box 299
Carthage, IL 62321-0299

The purchase of this book entitles the buyer to reproduce student activity pages for classroom use only. Any other use requires the written permission of Good Apple, Inc.

All rights reserved. Printed in the United States of America.

Table of Contents

Baggage Check 1
   Bulletin Boards 2
   "Mobile"ize Your Room 4

Passenger Pickup 6
   A FRIENDasaurus 7
   You Gotta Have Heart 15
   Secret Pal 19
   Let the Good Times Roll 22
   Our Gang 25
   Class Reunion 27
   Children's Day 31

Scenic Route 33
   Fair with a Flair 34
      City (Friendsville) 37
      Country (Jellostone) 40
      Beach (Ft. Waterdale) 43
      Amusement Park (Dizzy Land) .. 46
   Travel Tips 49
   Travel Brochure 50
   Vacation Planner 51

Tune Up 52
   Tune Up Your Body 53
   Tune Up Your Mind 55

Pit Stop 60
   Pack-a-Lunch Writing Center 61
      The Ripe Bunch 63

   Sweet Dreams 66
   Basket Case Mysteries 69
   Quenchers 72
   Footlong Stories 75
   A Tasty Choice 78

Adventure Venture 81
   Travellin' Packets 82
      Language Arts 84
      Writing 87
      Science 91
      Television 94
      Math 96
      Physical Education 99
      Art 101
      Music 104
      Share Time 108
   Junior Job Journal 111
      Application 119
   Summertime Rap 120

Sailing Away 129
   Digging Up 130
   Mapmaker 131
   Let's "Sail"ebrate 132
   Program 137
   Awards 141

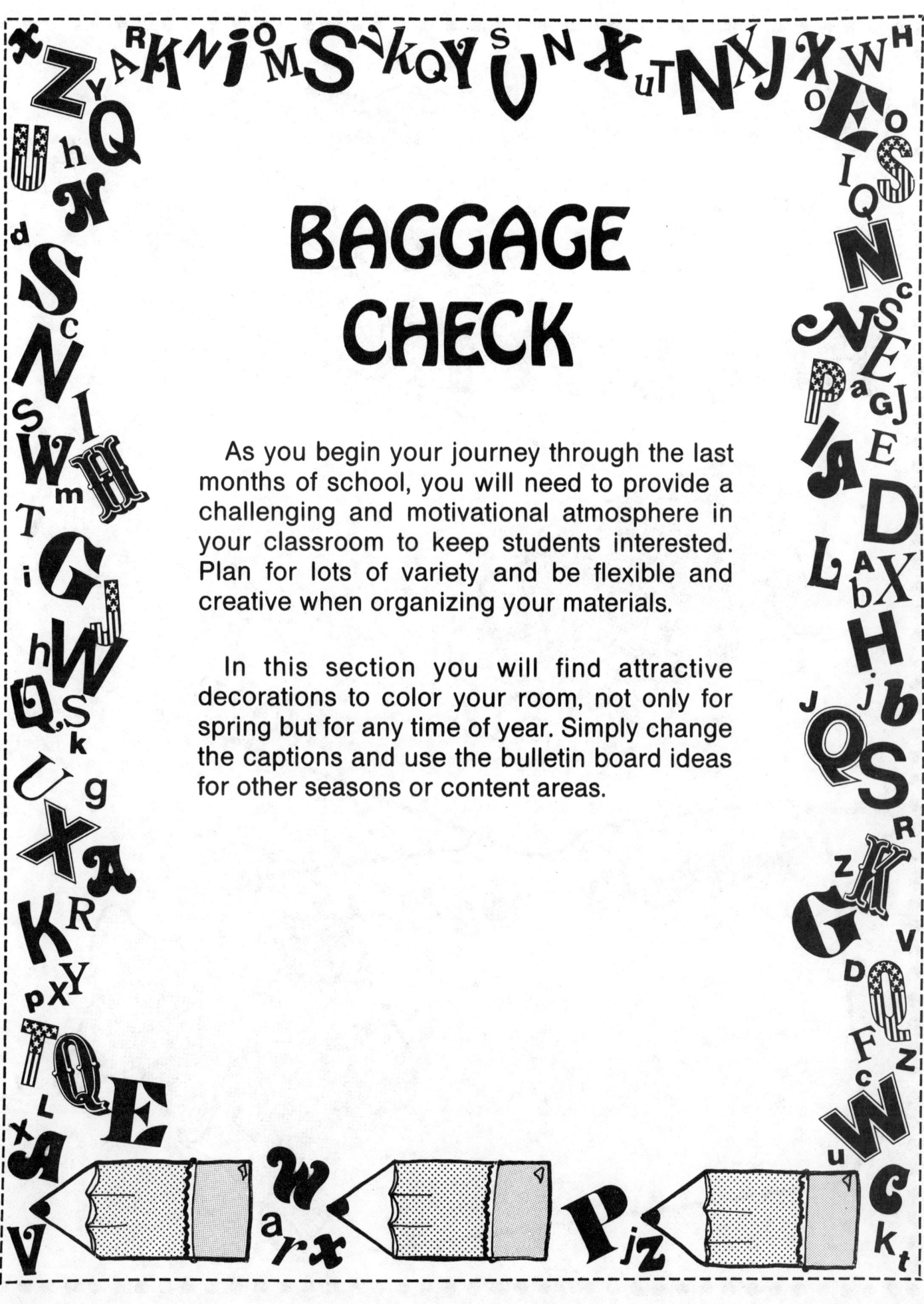

BAGGAGE CHECK

As you begin your journey through the last months of school, you will need to provide a challenging and motivational atmosphere in your classroom to keep students interested. Plan for lots of variety and be flexible and creative when organizing your materials.

In this section you will find attractive decorations to color your room, not only for spring but for any time of year. Simply change the captions and use the bulletin board ideas for other seasons or content areas.

END OF YEAR BULLETIN BOARDS

MOVIN' ON...

School's Out

RDS

We're Making Tracks

FORECASTING...

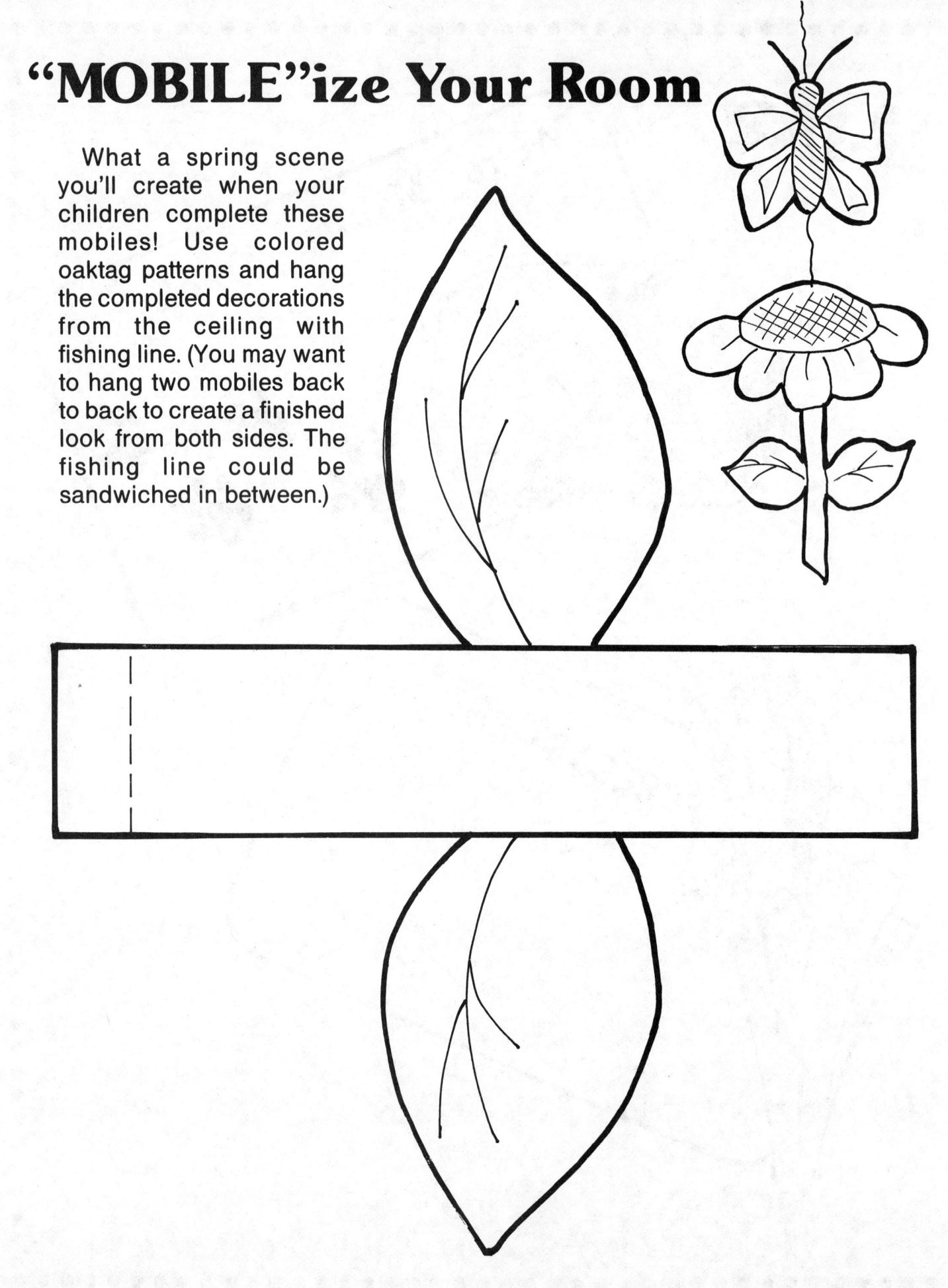

"MOBILE"ize Your Room

What a spring scene you'll create when your children complete these mobiles! Use colored oaktag patterns and hang the completed decorations from the ceiling with fishing line. (You may want to hang two mobiles back to back to create a finished look from both sides. The fishing line could be sandwiched in between.)

Copyright © 1990, Good Apple, Inc.

4

GA1145

Mobile Patterns

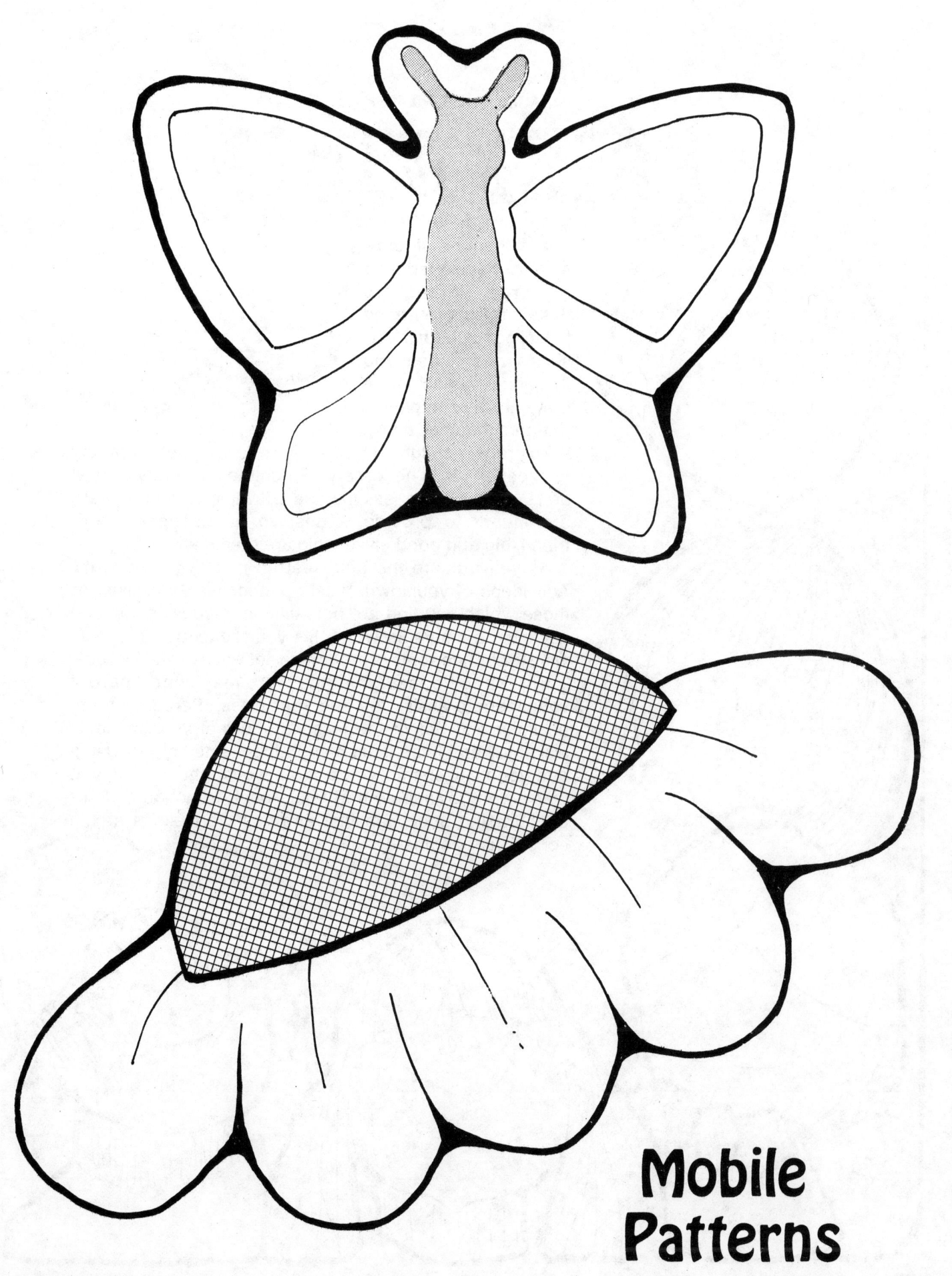

PASSENGER PICKUP

FRIENDSHIP

The theme of friendship is developed and reinforced throughout this unit. Children need to feel good about themselves and understand their inner values before they can find compatible partners that they enjoy.

To prepare children for an active role in society, a variety of experiences is necessary to promote individual as well as team effort. The lessons and activities presented here are meant to provide a positive atmosphere where friendship and good citizenship are practiced.

As you prepare the unit, keep in mind *your* students. Add ideas of your own, delete unnecessary activities or those which you find are not suitable to your needs, and establish a timetable which fits your schedule. You may wish to change some of the written activities to oral lessons.

For specific assignments you may want parent volunteers to assist you and your class. (Parents love to be involved!) Select the lessons you feel your students will enjoy and keep them alert to the themes of friendship and good citizenship. Once you have taught the unit, you many want to include it in your "back-to-school" plans, encouraging good behavior and positive feelings as the school year begins.

Copyright © 1990, Good Apple, Inc.

GA1145

A FRIENDasaurus

To create this bulletin board

Materials:
light-blue paper for background
black paper for lettering
green or brown paper for a FRIENDasaurus
brown butcher paper or construction paper rolled into overlapping segments for the tree
green construction paper for several large leaves
manila oaktag for the egg pattern (see page 9)
light-green oaktag for the FRIENDasaurus pattern (see page 8)
paper fasteners (one per child)
the name of each child written on a small piece of paper

Directions:
1. Place the lettering, tree, and FRIENDasaurus on the bulletin board.
2. Give each student an egg, a FRIENDasaurus pattern, and a paper fastener.
3. After each child draws the name of a classmate, explain to the children that they must keep the names drawn a secret. On the outside of the eggs, they must list clues about the persons drawn. (Encourge children to write positive compliments concerning good citizenship/friendship.) On FRIENDasaurus, they will write the name of the student described. Have children attach the egg to the FRIENDasaurus with the paper fastener and attach to the bulletin board.
4. Display completed projects on the bulletin board and let children solve the riddles.

A FRIENDasaurus Pattern

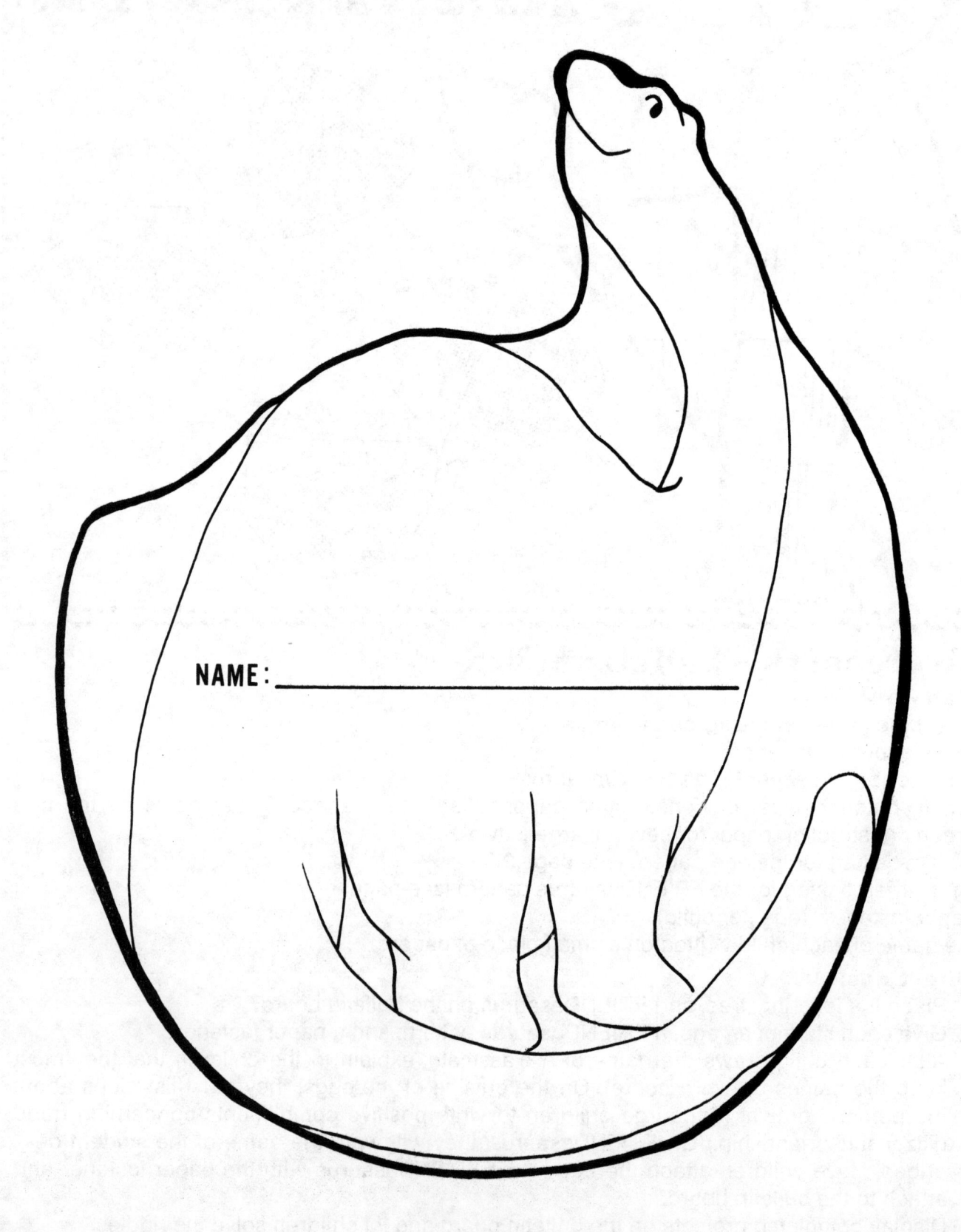

NAME: _____

CLUES

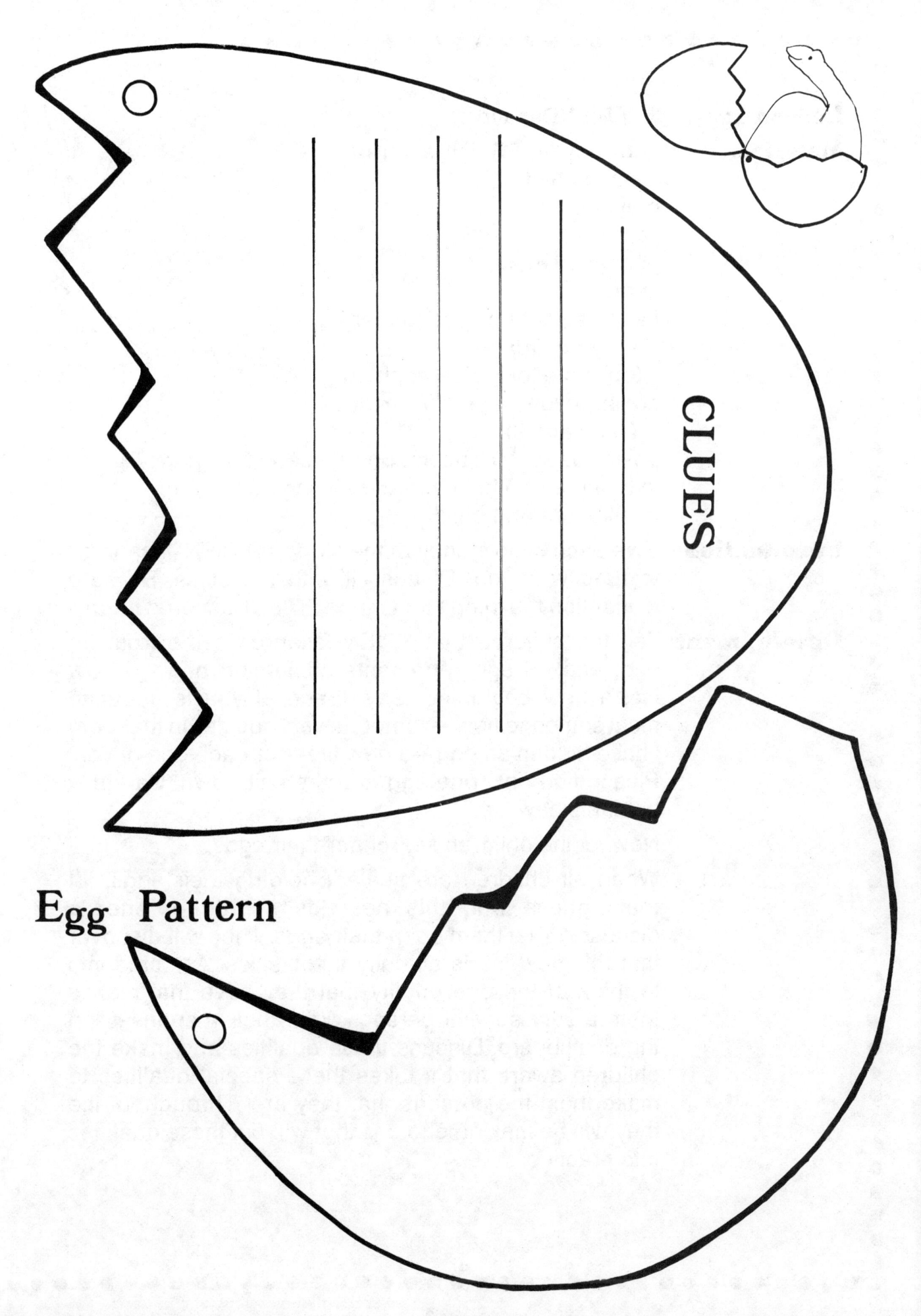

Egg Pattern

Lesson 1: "A FRIENDasaurus"

Materials: copy of "A FRIENDasaurus" for each child
crayons
scissors
paper fasteners
pencil
Leggs eggs or plastic Easter eggs (1 per child)
"You" note for inside each egg
construction paper for art lesson (see page 9)
poster paper for bulletin board scene (see page 7)
lettering for bulletin board (see page 7)
chalkboard and chalk

Introduction: Give each child a copy of the story "A FRIENDasaurus" to read with you. Discuss it with the class. Be sure to mention the things that made FRIENDasaurus happy.

Development: Tell the children that FRIENDasaurus came from an egg, and an egg represents something new—a new life, a new beginning. Say "Each of you is about to meet someone new—someone very special. In the room I have hidden an egg—a new life—for each one of you. Please find only one egg and then sit down. Carefully hold this new life."

Now let the children search for their eggs.

When all children are seated, holding their eggs, let them guess who this new life might be. After a discussion, let them open their eggs. They will discover that this new life is actually themselves. Ask students to think of the one quality that they have that makes them a very special person. Write their responses on the chalkboard. Discuss these qualities and make the children aware that it takes these special qualities to make them the persons that they are. Throughout life they will be making choices that will put these qualities into practice.

Copyright © 1990, Good Apple, Inc.

GA1145

Conclusion: Give each child a copy of the FRIENDasaurus art lesson (see page 9). Have him/her follow the directions given to complete the lesson. When the projects are finished, collect them for display on the bulletin board. Refer to the bulletin board throughout your study of friendship.

Hints: After students read the story "A FRIENDasaurus," let them add to the illustrations and color them at this time, or suggest that they complete the art at a later date during the unit.

Hide the eggs with the "you" notes inside prior to the lesson. You may want to hide them in another room in the building, your classroom, or in each child's desk. Put the bulletin board up before you begin teaching the unit so that the art projects can be added as students complete them. It will also add atmosphere to your room.

Today and throughout the unit (year) stress to your children that each of them has qualities that are good. Always remind students that they have something valuable to give others, whether it is a physical or mental attribute. A positive self-concept reinforced by you will create a warm, pleasant atmosphere where learning can occur. Continue to remind the children that they are like that new egg, capturing new experiences each day and growing a little at a time.

Use two sessions to complete this lesson if you feel that your children need two settings. The art lesson could easily be moved to the next day. Encourage children to talk about their good points. At the same time, advise them on ways to improve.

A FRIENDasaurus

1

It was dark. I felt cramped. I wanted to stretch my legs. They had been curled up for a long, long time. My chin was resting on my chest and I couldn't straighten my neck. If only it would get light. Then I could see where I was and get myself out of this place.

10

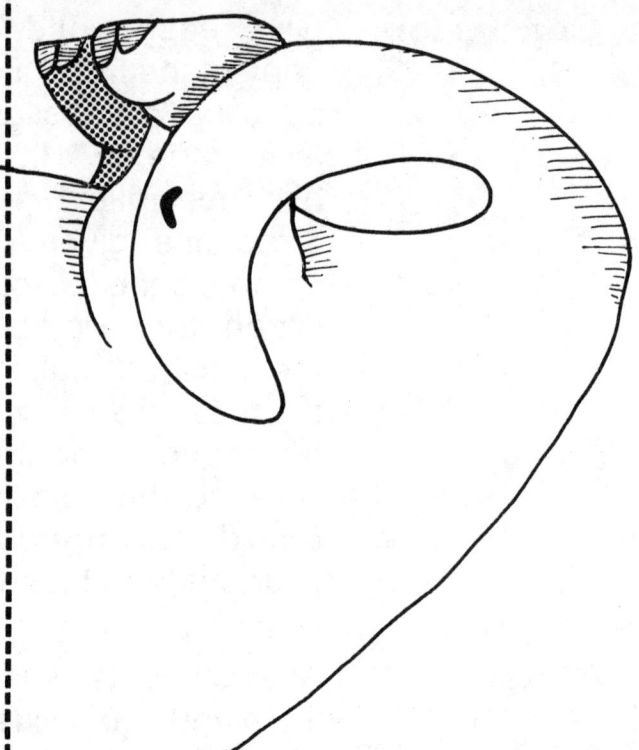

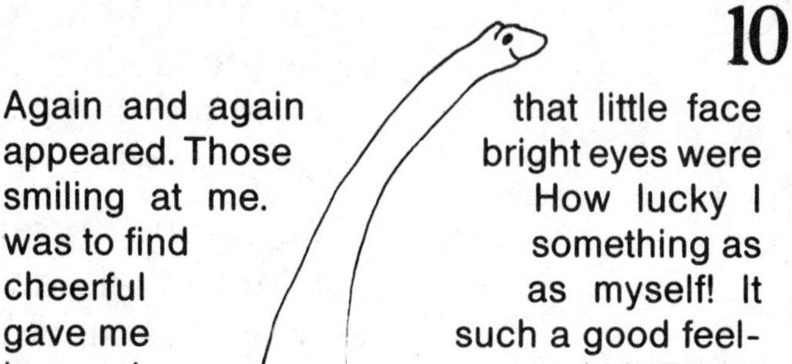

If I wanted to play, it was enthusiastic. If I felt sleepy, it was patient. If I was sad, it was understanding. But what was this THING? I felt as though I needed to give it a name! I thought and thought. Frienda? Frienda? How 'bout a FRIENDasaurus, just like me! I danced excitedly in the water.

11

"And do you know what I like best about a Frienda? I know that I can always count on him!"

Again and again appeared. Those smiling at me. was to find cheerful gave me ing, and that little face bright eyes were How lucky I something as as myself! It such a good feel- I LIKED IT.

Copyright © 1990, Good Apple, Inc.   12   GA1145

3

Thud! I came to a sudden stop. I heard something. CRACK! My body pushed through an opening and I could wiggle my legs a bit. My head was lying in soft, green grass and I felt wet as I squirmed to get loose. A bright light was shining down upon me and tall things were waving overhead. I lay still and waited. How warm my body was getting! I closed my eyes to enjoy the feeling.

8

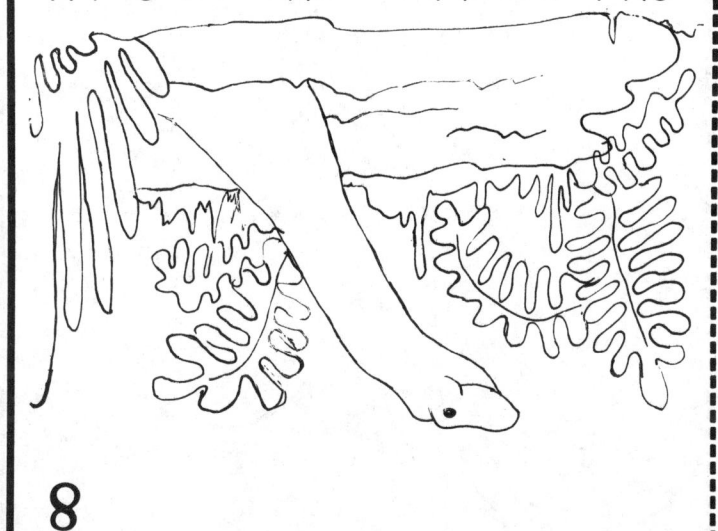

Oh! I stepped in something wet. Squish! Squish! Slowly I backed up. "What was that?" I questioned. I tiptoed forward and tried to feel that "shiny spot" with my nose. It wiggled! My nose got wet. Something was moving by my feet. My tail was covered and my legs were sinking. When I lowered my head, the shape in front of me got bigger. Scared, I ran up the hillside and hid. Cautiously I waited.

2

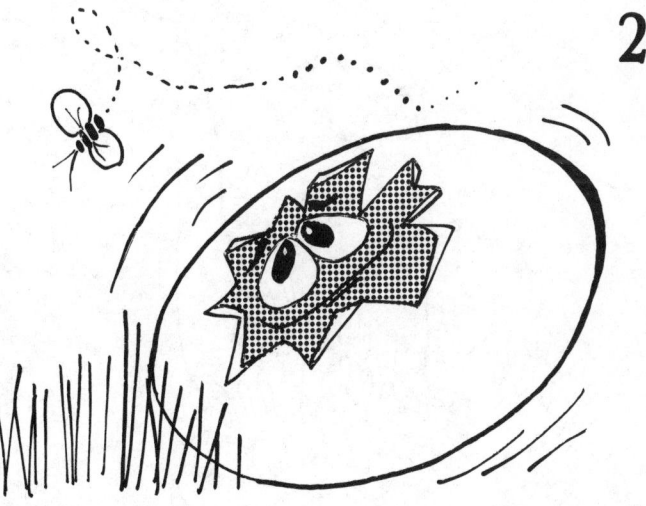

Just then I began spinning round and round. I was rolling and I was getting very, very dizzy. What was happening? Where was I going?

9

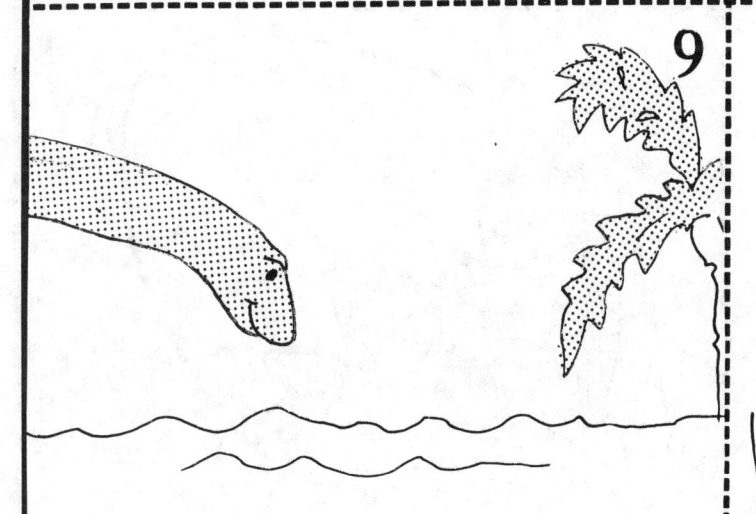

Slowly, back down the hill I crept. My eyes were fastened to the ground. There it was again! It was watching me with staring eyes. I paused. It didn't run away. It stayed. It seemed to want to play with me. When I moved, it came too! And when I stopped, those eyes stopped to watch again. If this was a game, I liked it!

Copyright © 1990, Good Apple, Inc.   13   GA1145

4

I must have fallen asleep, for when I awoke, the light was almost beside me on the ground and the shapes around me were fading. My eyes wandered from side to side as I snuggled deeper into my new bed. I lay very still. I waited.

5

There was that warm light again, shining in my eyes! I rolled over and tried to balance my short legs with my tail. Slowly I lifted my head. That was pretty simple! Carefully I stepped, a little shaky at first. I practiced walking all morning, and by afternoon, I felt rather confident.

6

What was that noise? Something inside of me rumbled. My tummy ached. It didn't take me long to discover that those tall, green shapes were tasty. Soon all of the low leaves were gone, but so was my energy. I was so, so tired. "Perhaps I'll just rest here a moment," I thought.

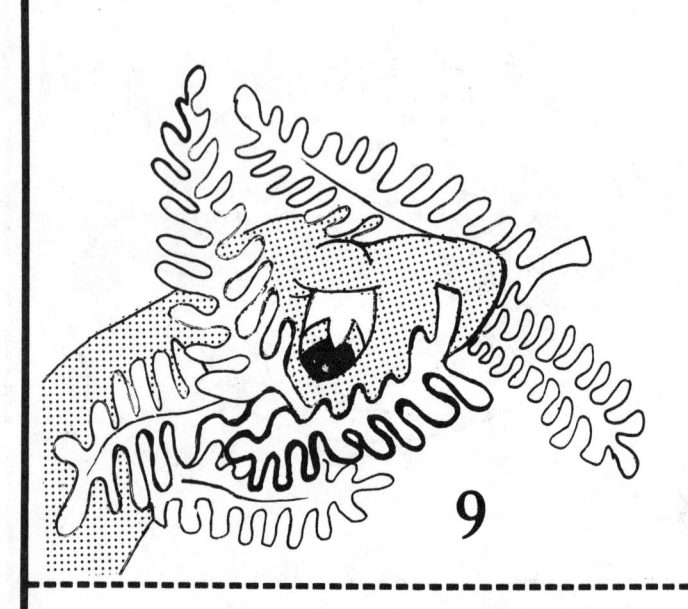

7

Tickle! Tickle! I scratched my nose on a stem and sat up. How long had I been sleeping? I jumped up and scampered along the path. My curious eyes were searching everywhere.

Lesson 2: "YOU GOTTA HAVE HEART"

Materials: heart stickers in a variety of colors or styles (one sticker per child)
creative dramatics cards (see next page)
envelope with puzzle pieces in it for each group (see page 18)

Introduction: Using four to six styles or colors of heart stickers, place one sticker on each student. Now seat your children in the room according to the kind of sticker each is wearing. Your class is now divided into teams for creative dramatics.

Development: Remind your students that they must work as a team. You have 20 creative dramatics cards for your children to role-play. Give each team a card and a two to five-minute time limit. When practice
time is over, let each team present its problem and solution to the rest of the class. Continue using the cards until all ideas have been presented. In some cases, not all students on the team are necessary for the solution. However, try to encourage all children to become involved.

Conclusion: To reinforce the concept of teamwork, give each group an envelope with a puzzle in it to solve. You may want the children to work in silence, communicating only with gestures.

Hints: Role-play problems your class might be having.
Teach the song "Make New Friends."
Assign team projects a few times each month to get the children used to working with others. Change teams often for variety.

1. You have just moved to a new neighborhood. You will be going to a new school. Suggest ways you could get acquainted with other children.

2. Your first grade neighbor is having a hard time adjusting to school. Describe several ways you could help this young student.

3. One of the students in your class seems to have no friends. What are some things you could do to help him/her?

4. The children in your class are calling you names. What can you do about it?

5. A close friend of yours constantly buys you presents. Some of them are pretty expensive. Although you like the gifts, you cannot afford to buy presents for her/him. How can you solve the problem?

6. A new student has enrolled in your school and is becoming a good friend of yours. Some of your old friends don't want her included in your group. What will you do?

7. One of your friends borrows things from you often. Rarely are they returned. How can you encourage the friendship, but reduce the borrowing?

8. A good friend wants to keep you all to himself/herself. You have several friends and enjoy the company of them all. What are your choices?

9. You find out that a friend of yours is having a party, but you have not been invited. How will you react to this?

10. Your best friend has moved away. How will you handle the situation?

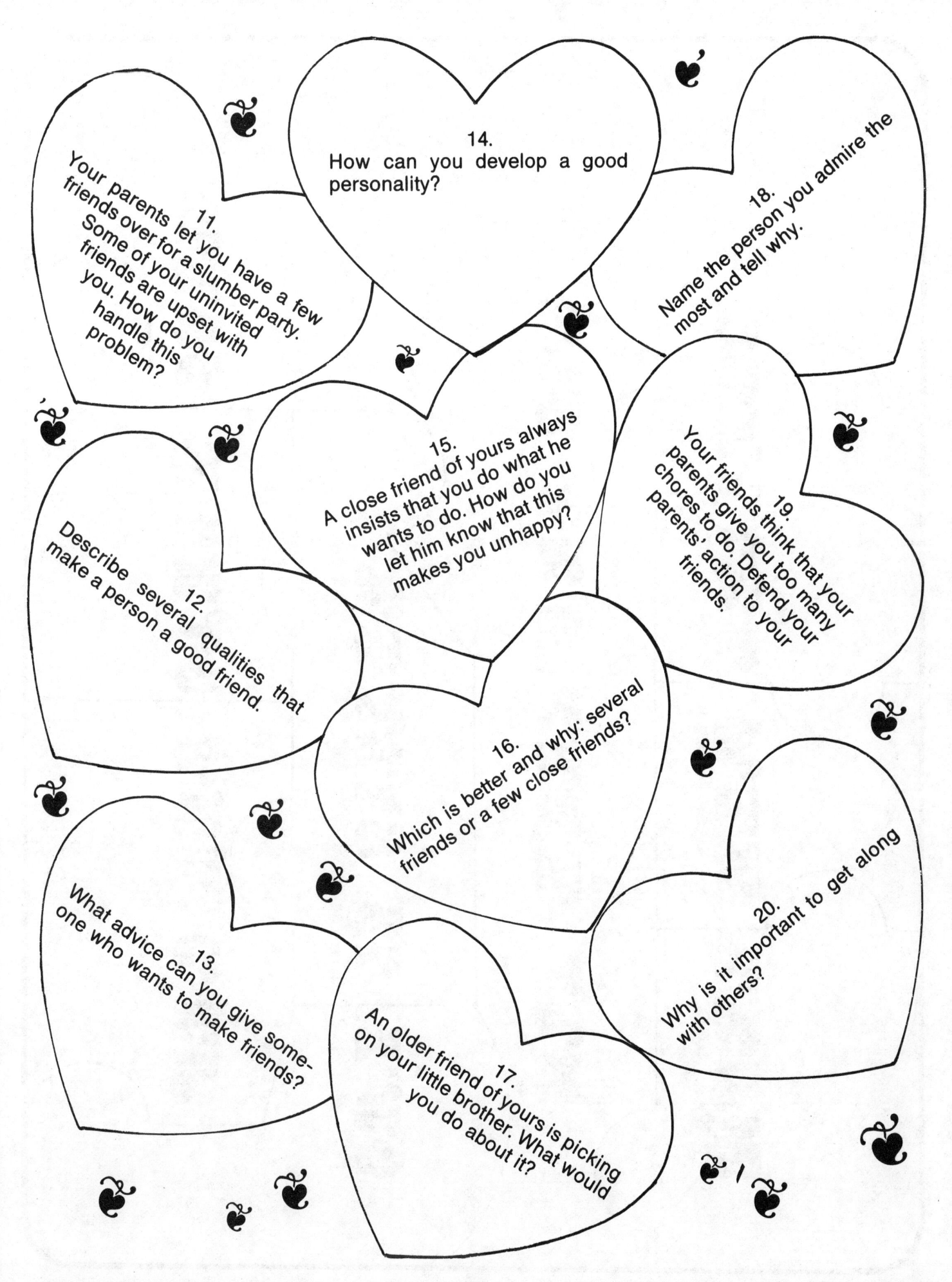

11. Your parents let you have a few friends over for a slumber party. Some of your uninvited friends are upset with you. How do you handle this problem?

14. How can you develop a good personality?

18. Name the person you admire the most and tell why.

12. Describe several qualities that make a person a good friend.

15. A close friend of yours always insists that you do what he wants to do. How do you let him know that this makes you unhappy?

19. Your friends think that your parents give you too many chores to do. Defend your parents' action to your friends.

13. What advice can you give someone who wants to make friends?

16. Which is better and why: several friends or a few close friends?

17. An older friend of yours is picking on your little brother. What would you do about it?

20. Why is it important to get along with others?

MAKE NEW FRIENDS, BUT KEEP THE OLD. ONE IS SILVER AND THE OTHER GOLD.

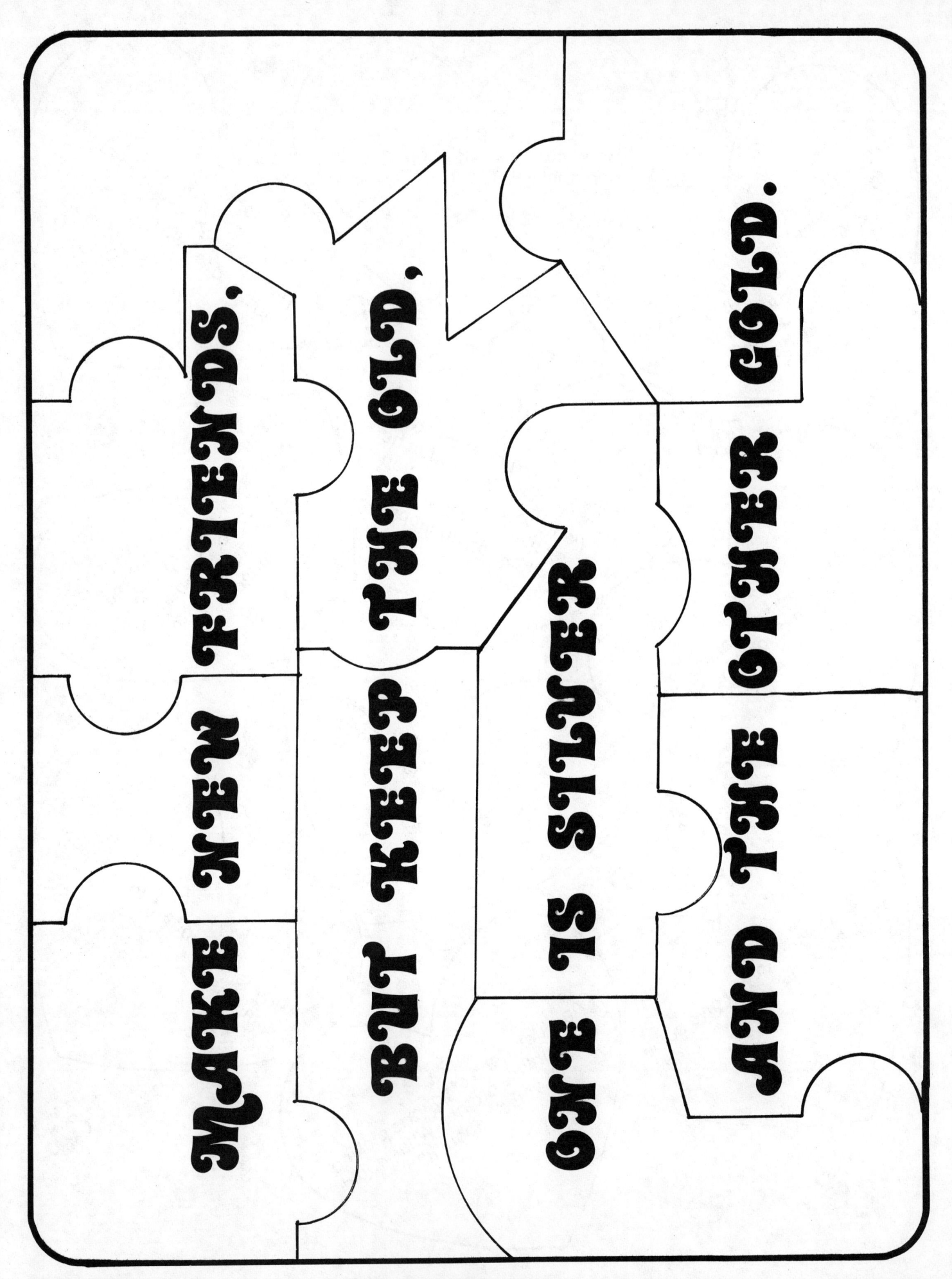

Lesson 3: "SECRET PAL"

Materials: name of each student written on a small piece of paper
small basket to hold the names
secret pal card for each child
"Secret Pal Projects" sheet (see page 21)

Introduction: Explain to your class that today they each will get a very special friend—a special pal. Throughout the day they will be doing special things for that secret person. Remind them to keep the name of that person secret! Put the names of all students in a small basket and let each child select a name. Now the fun begins!

Development: Give each student a secret pal card. Have him/her color the card and write a message to his/her secret pal sometime during the day. The last section of the card is an observation diary to be completed by the person to whom the card was given and returned to the sender. Allow time for the students to make projects to give to their secret pals during the day.

Conclusion: Have children complete various activities suggested during the day and secretly give them to their secret pals. Stress positive feelings in cases where they have conflicting personalities. At the end of the day ask each student to guess who his/her secret pal was.

Hints: Extend the time limit if children seem to be enjoying the secret pal idea.
Let children suggest activities of their own.

STARring My Secret Pal

I have watched you all day long while in my heart you played a song!

How nice of you to think of me! Lasting may our friendship be.

Duplicate this card for each student in your class to color, decorate, sign the middle portion and deliver to his/her secret pal. After receiving it, the secret pal should cut apart the bottom section and return it to the sender. Additional comments may be made on the reverse side.

Copyright © 1990, Good Apple, Inc. 20 GA1145

SECRET PAL PROJECTS

1. Send a singing telegram.
2. Make or bring a snack or his/her favorite treat.
3. Make a friendship bracelet.
4. Sit by him/her during the day.
5. Design an T-shirt or a bandana for him/her.
6. Pot a plant or flower.
7. Call him/her on the phone.
8. Play a game together during recess or free time.
9. Carry his/her books.
10. Share a joke.
11. Read him/her a story.
12. Draw or paint a picture.
13. Surprise him/her with a visit.
14. Invite him/her to a movie, to go skating, or to visit at your house.
15. Make a puzzle with a secret message on it.
16. Create a friendship basket (Baggie) filled with special treasures from you.
17. Share a happy, funny, or embarrassing experience you've had.
18. Send a diary about him/her from your observations or conversations.
19. Write him/her a poem or story.
20. Take a picture and give it to him/her in a frame you've designed.

Lesson 4: "LET THE GOOD TIMES ROLL"

Materials: checklist for good citizenship for each child
your favorite play dough recipe (one that can be baked or be made into a permanent shape)
ingredients and materials for making play dough
construction paper for skate patterns (see page 24)
scissors
yarn or heavy string
glue
toothpicks (one per child)
safety pins (one per child)

Introduction: Give each student the checklist for good citizenship (see page 23). Review and discuss it with your class.

Development: Bring your play dough recipe, ingredients, and materials to school for your children to make friendship beads. If you prefer, make the play dough before the lesson, and have it ready to use. Ask each child to make 5-20 beads from the dough, using a shape he/she chooses. Insert the toothpick through the center of each bead to make a hole. The completed beads can then be placed on string as the art lesson suggests.

Conclusion: Explain to your students that you want them to observe their fellow classmates for good citizenship. When they notice someone who displays one of the ideas suggested on the checklist, they should give that person one bead to place on his/her roller skate.

Hints: Make several colors of play dough for variety. Ask the children to help you create a checklist for good citizenship.
Place a hole in each bead with a toothpick before the dough hardens.

Good Citizenship

Webster defines *citizenship* as the duties, rights and privileges of this status. As you initiate this discussion about citizenship in your classroom, record and discuss these three areas with your students. Brainstorm first with your students, and use the ideas presented to supplement the discussion.

DUTIES:
1. To learn to work individually as well as in a group
2. To accept responsibility for ourselves when working or playing
3. To follow rules/laws established by the government, by our school administration, by our class, by our clubs, and by our parents (Rules protect personal property, public property, and ourselves.)

RIGHTS/PRIVILEGES:
Most schools have a students' rights handbook. Refer to this guide when discussing this area with your class. Explain to the children that by accepting our duties, we earn certain rights.

Discuss the fact with the children that by practicing rules established by our parents, teachers, students, and other adults, we learn to make wise decisions. These rules help us solve problems. As we grow older, our rules continue to change, enabling us to accept more responsibilities and earn more rights/privileges. By practicing good citizenship we form values which will guide us in day-to-day living for the rest of our lives.

Mention that Boy Scouts, Girl Scouts, and 4-H stress good citizenship, as do various service/community clubs.

ROLLIN' ON......

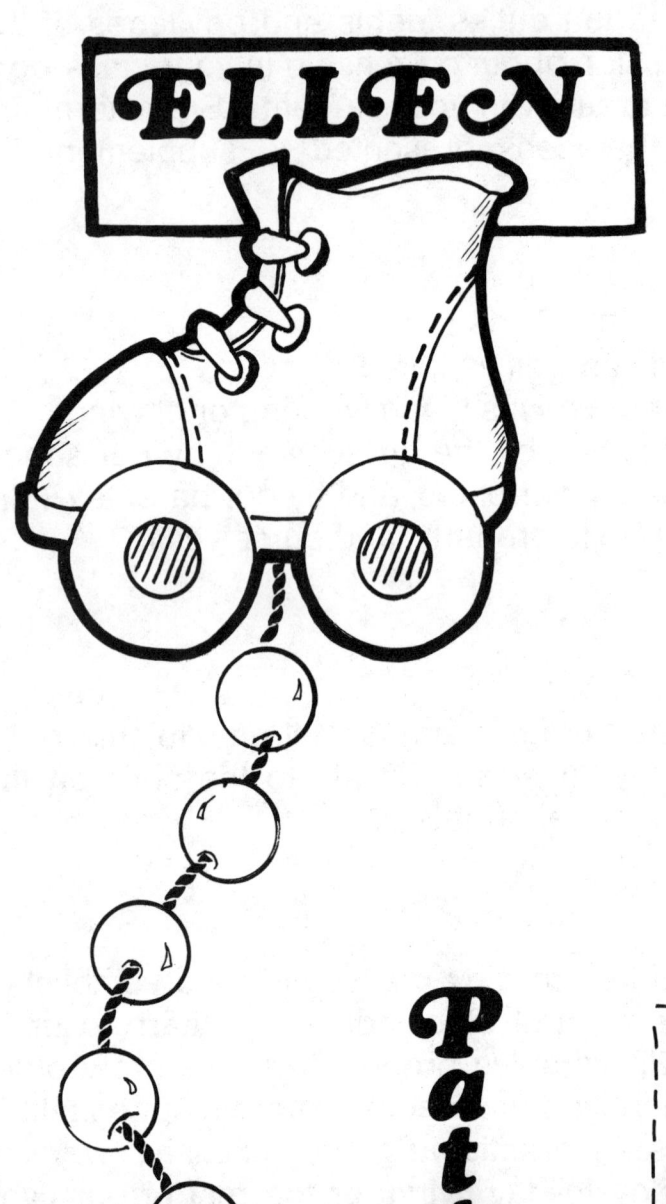

Provide each child with an oaktag copy of the roller skate pattern. Ask each child to write his/her name in large letters at the top. Poke a small hole in the bottom part of the roller skate and attach a piece of yarn. Use a safety pin to hold the skate on each child's shirt.

Ask each child to make 5-20 dough beads using your favorite recipe. Before the dough hardens, have children poke a hole with their toothpick through the center of each bead. In this way the beads can be strung onto the yarn. Tie a small knot in the yarn under each bead to hold it in place.

Discuss the idea of *citizenship* with your students prior to this activity, or perhaps while the dough beads are baking or hardening. Tell children that they will be observing their classmates carefully. When they witness a kind act, they may present a bead of theirs to that child as they remind that child of the specific gesture. Examples: "Trisha, that was kind of you to get Sarah's homework together when she got sick." "Sandra, thanks for letting Melissa borrow your pencil."

You, the teacher, may also want to make beads. Watch for those children who are not getting beads and try to reward them for something special.

Pattern

Lesson 5: "OUR GANG"

Materials: approximately 12-20 foot roll of bulletin board paper or mural paper
glue
scissors
yarn, fabric, lace, ribbon, or other sewing notions
large paper plates (one per student) for faces
pencils, crayons, markers, or paint
oaktag or construction paper for clothing, hair, accessories

Introduction: Explain to the children that they will be making a wall mural. Show students that the large paper will be the "body" and that they will create their faces from paper plates, adding features and decorations that they choose (see next page).

Development: Give each child the appropriate materials to complete his/her part of the banner. Demonstrate the project to the class. Allow time for children to explore decorative possibilities when designing their own person.

Conclusion: Display the banner itself while students are working. As they finish their project, add faces and hands to the banner. Ask each child to write his/her name on the banner, perhaps along with a message to others, or to display a good paper or other designated assignment on the banner below his/her artwork.

Hints: Display the finished banner in the classroom or hallway for others to see.
Use the banner as an end-of-school graffiti poster. Let children take turns writing farewell wishes on it.
Hang the banner on the first day of school as a welcome-back-to-school art lesson.
Select a title to place above the banner. Suggestions include: "Our Gang," "Class Reunion," "Class of 19___," "Farewell," "Welcome, Class."

OUR GANG

Lesson 6: "CLASS REUNION"

Materials: copies of the class booklet for each child (see page 28)
pencil
crayons
markers
scissors
chalk/chalkboard

Introduction: Reminisce about the year that you and your class have just spent together. Ask a class officer or a student with good handwriting/spelling to record memories discussed on the chalkboard. Perhaps mention favorite activities in sequential order by months, class projects, fairs, or contests.

Development: Provide each child with a copy of the class reunion booklet. Review it with your class, suggesting that they incorporate ideas written on the chalkboard during brainstorming. Tell the children that after they color, cut out, and staple their booklet together, there will be several blank pages. It is on these pages that they can record a class list, phone numbers, addresses, birthdays, class officers, favorite clubs, autographs, comments, and pictures. (An alphabetical class list on the board might be helpful prior to the lesson for children to copy.)

Conclusion: Allow time for classmates to exchange comments, information, and enjoyment as they complete the activities in the class reunion booklet.

Hints: Personalize activities in the booklet by listing ideas of your own.
Remind students to take the booklet home to refer to during summer vacation.
Let children complete the booklet outside where they can visit and move freely.
Prior to the lesson, choose committees to provide entertainment, refreshments, and/or skits.

CLASS BOOKLET

NAME: _____

ABOUT MY SCHOOL

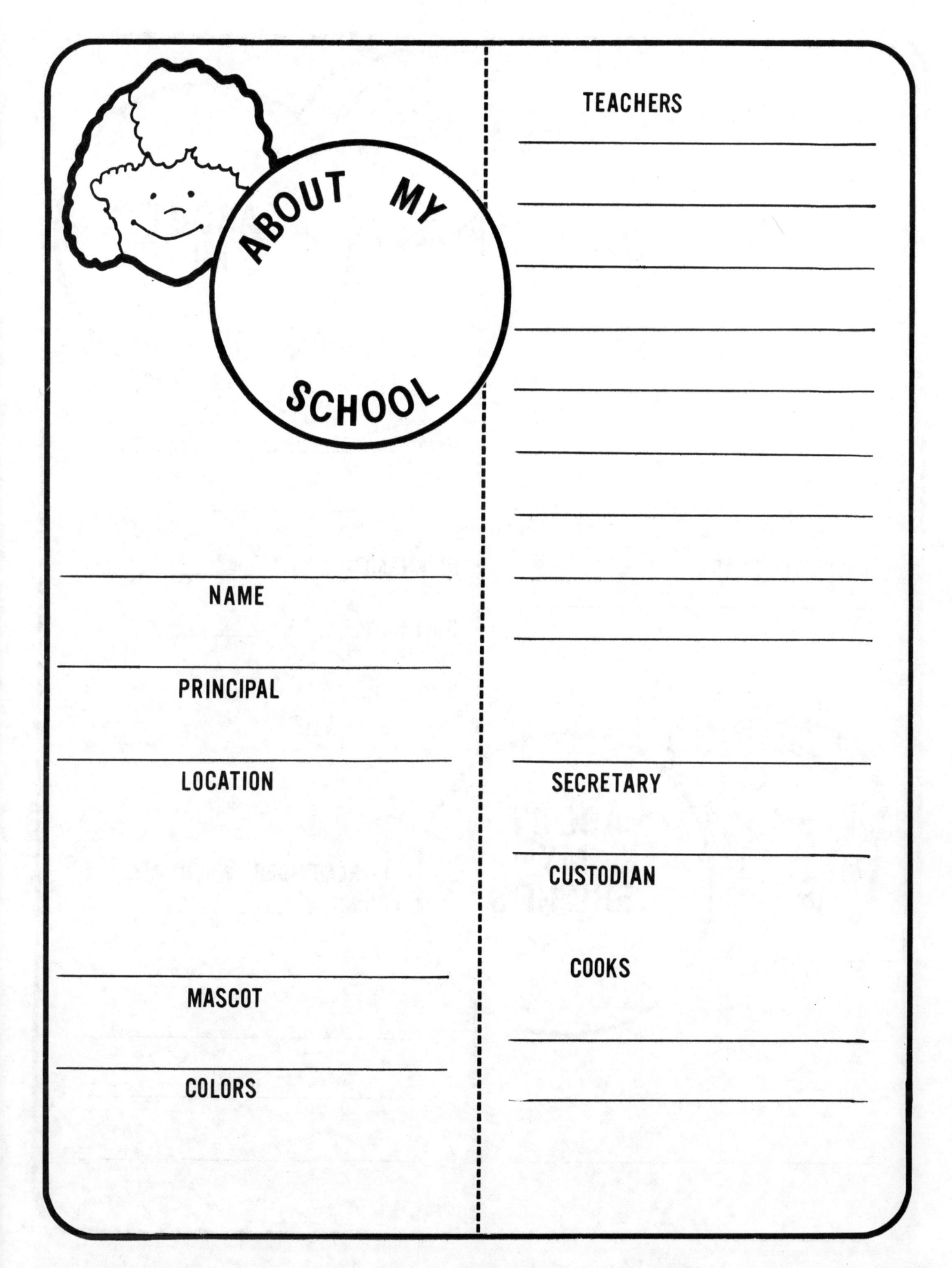

TEACHERS

_____

NAME

_____

PRINCIPAL

_____

LOCATION

_____

MASCOT

_____

COLORS

_____

SECRETARY

_____

CUSTODIAN

_____

COOKS

_____

MY CLASSES
_____
_____
_____
_____
_____
_____

FAVORITE CLASS
_____

ABOUT ME

NAME _____

_____

NICKNAME _____

BIRTHDAY _____

AGE _____

ABOUT MY FRIENDS

BEST FRIENDS
_____
_____
_____

I REMEMBER WHEN MY FRIEND _____
_____
_____
_____

Lesson 7: "CHILDREN'S DAY"

Materials: your students
parents, grandparents, relatives, children in the school

Introduction: Both May 1 and June 10 are known as Children's Day. Sometimes Children's Day is called Flower Day, Rose Day, or May Day. Regardless of when you choose to celebrate it, those honored are still the children—in your classroom or in other areas of the world. Set aside time to celebrate with your students!

Development: Use all the resources in your classroom to produce a program for others—parents, relatives, your school, or your community. With your students, plan activities which they will enjoy sharing. This could be an all-day event, or a short program during school or in the evening (total class participation should be a goal).

Conclusion: Use these ideas or those of your own:
1. Open House—During the day let parents observe their child in actual classroom experiences.
2. Tea—Let children host and plan this from beginning to end to encourage development of proper etiquette.
3. Exhibits—Display exhibits on a variety of content areas to stress the strengths of each student. Suggest oral or written projects.
4. Hall of Fame—Ask students to portray their favorite personalities by dressing in costumes and presenting brief speeches.

5. Program—Include reminiscing about the past year; present a slide show of the activities throughout the year; encourage recitation of poetry or famous speeches; provide instrumentation and choral experiences; present awards; perform dances.

Hints:
Encourage all students to participate in the selection and planning of events.

Provide ample time for rehearsal so that children feel comfortable and successful.

Promote a positive atmosphere where children can have fun while they prepare.

Select one or a combination of activities to make your celebration special.

Keep in mind that not all students may be able to participate if the celebration were to be an evening event.

Add a cultural flair to your program by including May Day traditions from foreign countries (songs in foreign languages, dances from other countries, decorations suggesting other areas of the world).

SCENIC ROUTE

Try these innovative approaches when teaching map skills to children. At an early age there are techniques that parents and teachers can use to make the map reading experiences fun. Make a small treasure hunt map. Begin by drawing a simple diagram of your child's room. Use lots of pictures. Place numbers on the diagram so that your child will know the sequence of events. Hide a small treasure or note at each station. When all notes have been found, reward the child in some way. This will provide a good incentive. Work with your child so that all directions are followed. Treasure hunts can progress from the child's room to the rest of the house or even around the yard at home or at school. Begin with familiar places so that the child relates to pictures of objects. After several successful treasure hunts, begin using a key on the map to replace the actual objects. In this way, the child will become familiar with abstract markings on maps.

With older students, experiment with various types of maps. Give them several outline maps of their state or country. With your guidance, let them make a political, physical, resource, or other map, being sure to label each. Have them create other types of maps they might suggest (rainfall, population, weather). Invite a cartographer to your classroom to talk with your students.

Display various types of maps in the classroom so that children can become comfortable with them. Allow time for children to touch the maps and locate places with a friend. Encourage children to draw maps or bring maps to school to show places they have vacationed. Remind parents to give children maps of places where they are travelling. Let them find route numbers and points of interest. Have students use magic markers to show progress as they travel. Ask children to calculate distances and make predictions for arrival time at various places. Allow children to plan for rest stops and/or meals. Encourage children to keep a diary to record specific information about their trip. (This could be used on a class field trip, also.) Bring in maps of fabulous vacation spots. Let children explore these individually or in groups and share what they have discovered with other children. Ask children to plan a "Fantasy Vacation" using maps, itinerary guides, expense accounts, travel tips, and so on. Invite a travel agent to your classroom to talk about making reservations, passports, packing, planning your agenda, and foreign currency.

FAIR WITH A FLAIR

Each year many older children are faced with creating projects for a social studies fair. This year have a "Fair with a Flair." Try a mini fair in your classroom. Just follow the simple steps listed below:

1. Give each student the Personality Test (page 35).

2. Place children into groups according to Personality Test results (A = City, B = Country, C = Beach, D = Amusement Park).

3. Give each child the appropriate folder of materials to complete. You may want to establish a contract for grades, for example: 8-10 projects = A; 6-7 = B. Suggest to the children that they may add or substitute activities of their own if they meet with your approval.

4. Allow ample time for students to work on projects. Provide resources such as maps, brochures, construction paper, and reference books for each group.

5. Organize a display area for each group. Use your classroom, library, or hallway. Label each City, Country, Beach, or Amusement Park.

6. Ask each group to display their materials in an appropriate manner. Music, audio-visuals, food, or token gifts might also be included.

7. Invite other children to the exhibits. You may want to choose a spokesperson from each group to explain the projects.

PERSONALITY TEST

Color in the answer that best describes you.

1. I would rather: a. tour a museum   b. mountain climb   c. relax in the sun   d. go through a haunted house

2. I enjoy: a. seeing lots of tall buildings   b. sitting by a quiet lake   c. playing in the sand   d. eating cotton candy

3. Sometimes I like to ride: a. in a car in traffic   b. in a canoe   c. on a surfboard   d. on a roller coaster

4. Sounds that I like to hear include: a. tooting horns   b. birds chirping   c. waves rolling   d. people laughing

5. A career that suits me might be: a. policeman   b. forest ranger   c. lifeguard   d. machine operator

6. A gift I would like to receive for my birthday might be: a. clothes   b. sneakers   c. scuba equipment   d. tickets for something

7. On my day off I would like to see: a. busy streets   b. green trees   c. lots of water   d. entertainment

8. My idea of fun would be to: a. have lunch on the top floor of a skyscraper   b. fish for trout   c. build a sand castle   d. sit with a friend at the top of a Ferris wheel

9. I don't mind: a. waiting for an elevator   b. sleeping outdoors   c. getting sand in my shoes   d. waiting in line

10. If I could choose somewhere special to live, I'd select: a. New York City   b. Yellowstone National Park   c. Malibu Beach   d. Disney World

To decide which vacation spot suits your personality, you must total the points earned. On the lines below record the number of times you selected each letter on your test.

a. _____   b. _____   c. _____   d. _____

If most of your points fell in: a—you should vacation in the CITY; b—you should spend time in the COUNTRY; c—you should relax at the BEACH; d—you should spend vacation time at an AMUSEMENT PARK.

GETTING STARTED

Now let's begin. Some children will bring experiences from many past family vacations to their group. Other students must fantasize about the fun they missed. Combine these personalities and let the children go.

A. File Folders—Give each student a manila file folder to decorate. Instruct the student to write his/her name on it and to keep all of the work in it.

B. Maps/Map Work Sheet/Projects—Give each child the appropriate map. The personality test will determine which children need city activities (Friendsville map/ activities/projects); country activities (Jellostone map/activities/projects); beach activities (Ft. Waterdale); or amusement park activities (Dizzy Land). Each child will have three work sheets. Assign children to work in city, country, beach, or amusement park groups. This will facilitate dispensing of information and materials.

***You may decide you would rather have all students complete all of the maps with you just for the experience of reading different types of maps and following directions. This would also give them exposure to different vacation possibilities. Then they could be placed in groups for specific study of a city, a place in the country, etc.

C. Travel Tips Information Sheet—You may choose to give these to children to review on their own, or discuss the tips orally. Let the children dramatize!

D. Travel Brochure—Have each child or group select a specific city, beach, or park to study in detail. Ask him/her to draw and color a travel poster or map on the back of the brochure and complete the information on the front. The tri-fold brochure will be complete.

E. Expense/Itinerary Form—Ask each child to complete this section. You may want to review it with your class before asking your students to plan.

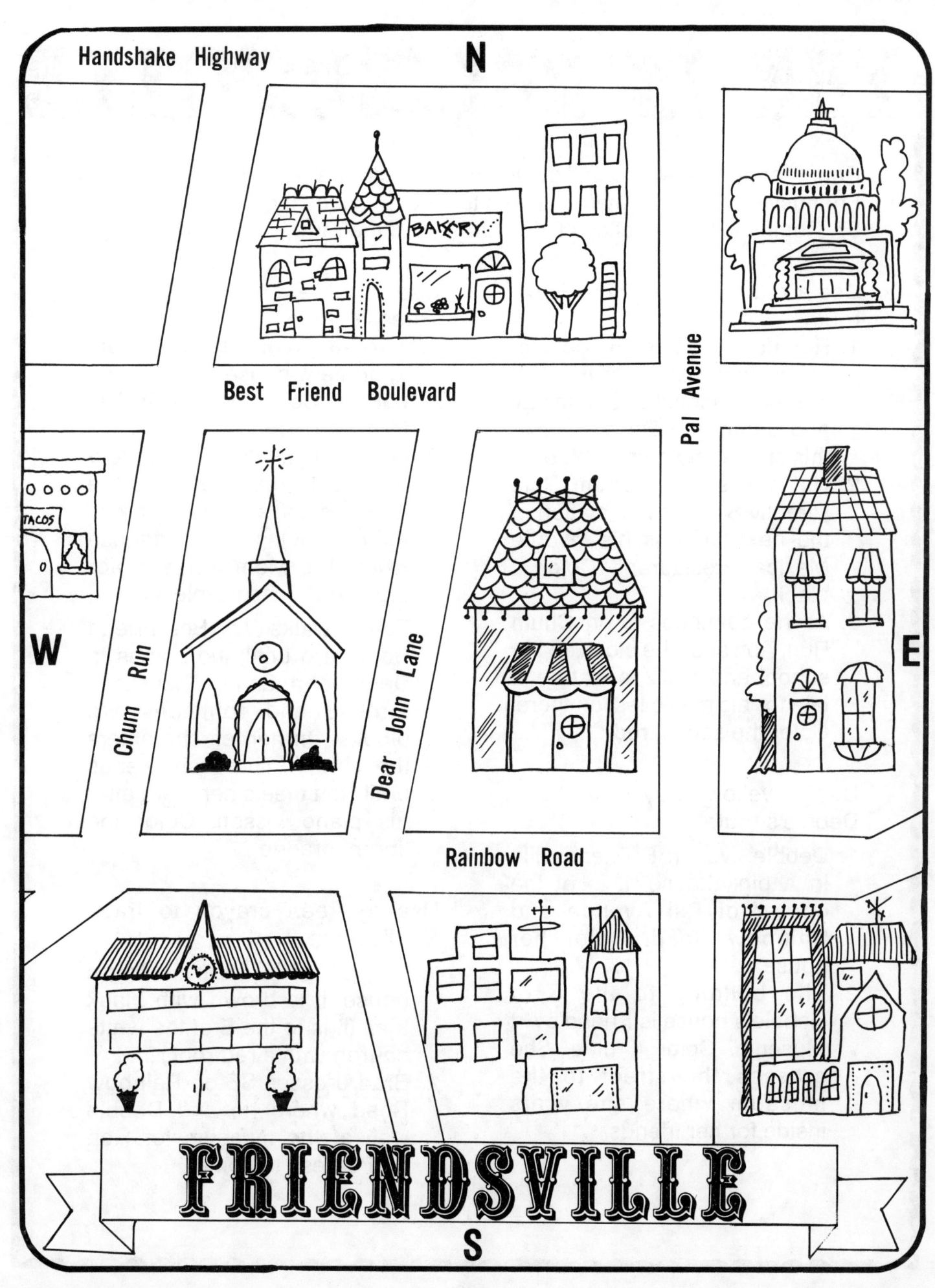

Handshake Highway

N

Best Friend Boulevard

Pal Avenue

W

Chum Run

Dear John Lane

E

Rainbow Road

FRIENDSVILLE

S

Copyright © 1990, Good Apple, Inc.

37

GA1145

FUN IN FRIENDSVILLE

Ron, Teresa, Brad, and Debbie want to spend the day together in Friendsville. They are making plans to meet by following the map on page 37. Complete the directions below and see if their trip is successful.

Use a red crayon to trace Ron's route.
1. Ron rides the bus and gets off at the bus station at the NW corner of Handshake Highway and Chum Run. Draw a bus in this space and color it blue.
2. He travels S on Chum Run. Directly S of the bus station in the next block is his favorite Mexican restaurant. Color it black.
3. As he continues S on Chum Run, Ron sees the clock on the school and realizes that he is late for his music lesson there. Color the school red.

Use a yellow crayon to trace Debbie's route.
1. Debbie lives in E Friendsville in a pink house. It is at the corner of Pal Avenue and Rainbow Road. Color her house.
2. The building to the S of Debbie's house is Friend's Art Museum. Color it blue. She crosses the street to the museum where she waits inside for her friends.

Use a blue crayon to trace Teresa's route.
1. Teresa lives in a yellow apartment house by a brown bakery. Color the tree in her front yard green.
2. On the other side of the bakery is an old green hotel. To the E of Teresa's house (across Pal Avenue) is the courthouse where her Mom works. Color the courthouse purple.
3. Teresa walks W on Best Friend Boulevard until she comes to Dear John Lane. There she turns S and continues two blocks. On her left she enters the library. There she reads until Ron meets her there after his piano lesson. Color the library orange.

Use a green crayon to trace Brad's route.
1. To the N of the library is Brad's house. It is brown with black trim. (It is to the E of the white church with a red roof.)
2. Brad crosses SE on Rainbow Road where he and Debbie wait at the museum for Ron and Teresa to come.

Projects to Do
ABOUT THE CITY

1. Make or collect objects which might be found in your city. Arrange these in a museum for others to see. Place small signs or labels by the objects to explain them (example: Michelangelo's Paintbrush).
2. Make a list of several businesses in your city. Choose one that you would like to learn more about. If possible, visit that business. If you cannot go there in person, write to them for information to use for your project. Or research that business in your library or through your travel agency. Arrange your information on poster board, in a small scrapbook, or in a display.
3. Write down several interesting places to visit in your city. Write a small paragraph about each of these places. Make your information interesting so that others will want to go there. Include pictures or drawings if possible.
4. Write a poem about your city. Include names of specific places to see or people you might meet. Copy this poem in your best writing and share it with others.
5. Select the name of someone famous from your city. Write his biography. Include pictures or objects which portray this person.
6. Build a model city. Use cardboard, boxes, construction paper, Legos, or anything else you might think of. Be sure to include the name of your city on the model. Label special places.
7. Teach the class a song or a game from your city.
8. Create a crossword puzzle about your city. You may include famous people, places, food, landmarks, or anything else you desire.
9. Get a map of your city from your travel agency or draw one of your own. Label important places. Be neat and accurate.
10. Interview a person from your city. Prepare a list of questions you want to ask that person. Record the answers and share the information.

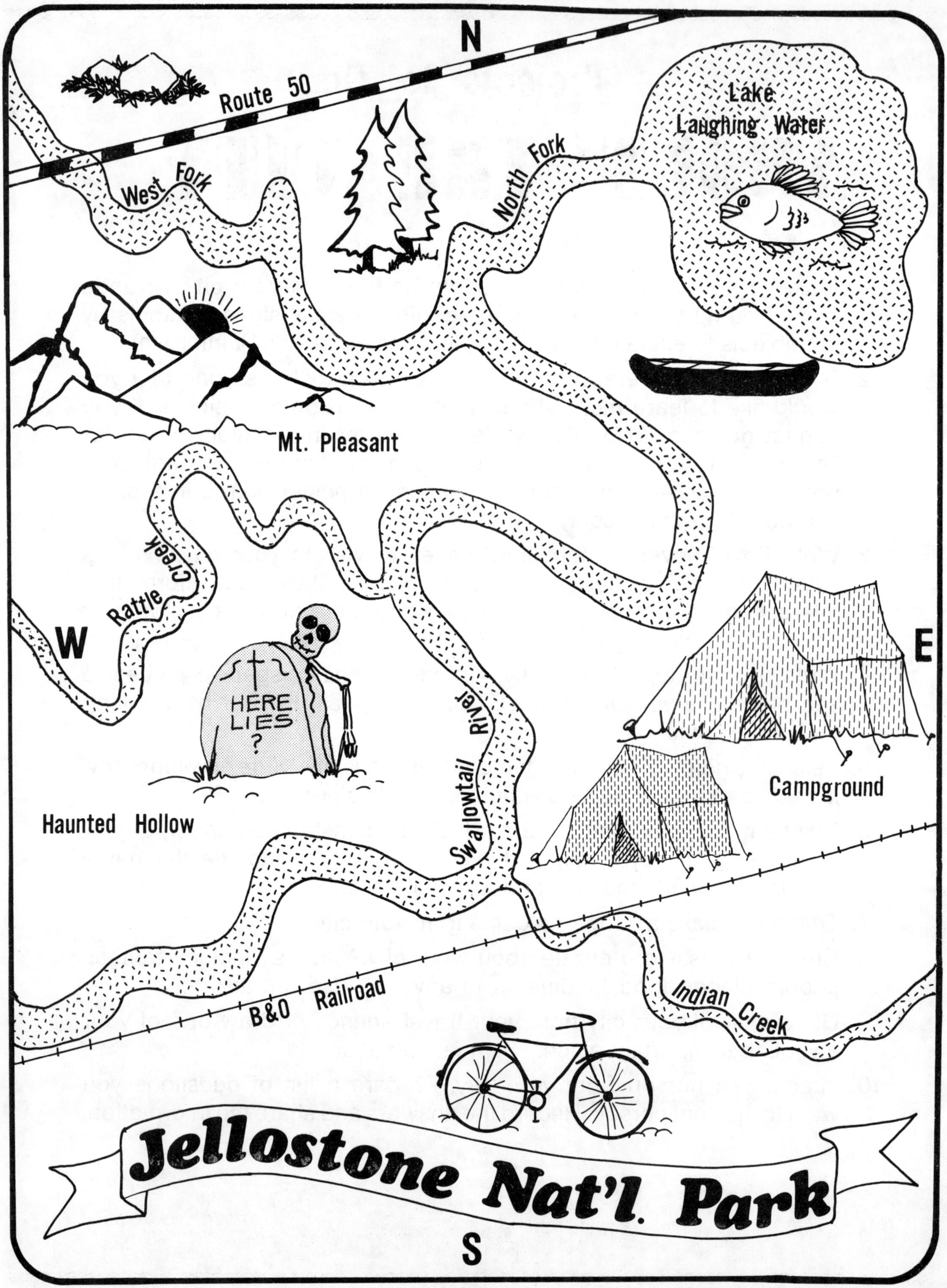
N
Route 50
Lake Laughing Water
West Fork
North Fork
Mt. Pleasant
Rattle Creek
W
E
HERE LIES ?
Swallowtail River
Campground
Haunted Hollow
B&O Railroad
Indian Creek
Jellostone Nat'l. Park
S

Joy at Jellostone

July 21, 1989

Dear Mom and Dad,

Camp is great. I like everything but the bugs. Those mosquitoes and granddaddy longlegs love my tent. I'm actually gaining weight. The food is gross, but my tent mate brought a duffel bag full of stuff from the 7-Eleven.

I can't believe I've only been here a week, and already I've had enough for a summer. Billy, my counselor, loves adventure, and he makes sure we do something neat every day.

I drew up a map of Camp Jellostone. When you get my letter, you can see for yourself what I mean by fun. I numbered and labeled the places for you.

Love,
Jeremy

P.S. Can I stay two weeks next summer?

Sunday:
1. We rode the bus along Route 50 and followed the West Fork to Swallowtail River. About halfway down Swallowtail River we pitched our tents. (Mine is the little one beside Billy's.)

Monday:
2. We got up at dawn and paddled our canoes up Swallowtail River to the North Fork. At Lake Laughing Water we caught our lunch. Later we swam and then headed back to camp.

Tuesday:
3. Wearing our backpacks we hiked to Pine Grove. We set up camp by the West Fork. It was so peaceful that we decided to stay until Thursday.

Thursday:
4. Leaving the West Fork campsite, we hiked to Mt. Pleasant where we stopped for lunch after a quick swim in Rattle Creek. The water was freezing, but so clear you could see every snake! At suppertime we stopped in Haunted Hollow to spend the night. Those ghost stories had me scared to death!

Friday:
5. We crossed Swallowtail River and followed the B & O Railroad back to camp, where we slept the rest of the day.

Saturday:
6. After breakfast by Indian Creek we decided to go for a creek hike. My new Nike's aren't so white anymore! In the afternoon Billy took us biking around our campground. Later that night we built a campfire near Billy's tent and sang songs. I felt pretty sad knowing I was coming home tomorrow.

Projects to Do
About the Country

1. Paint a picture showing what life in the country might be like.

2. Make a list of all the sports you can do in the country. Choose one sport to study in detail. Bring proper equipment and demonstrate this sport to your class. Perhaps play the sport during recess.

3. Write a story about the country. It can be an experience you have had or one that you have created.

4. Invite a forest ranger to speak to your class about forest fires, careers, hunting and fishing regulations, forest animals, recreation, or another area which you might find interesting.

5. Bring a topographical map and a compass to your class and explain to the children how they are used. If you don't feel comfortable explaining this information, ask a Boy/Girl Scout leader or other adult who might teach your class.

6. Find out about the state parks in your area. Choose one that seems interesting and tell your class about it.

7. Select a park anywhere in the world. Research it and set up a display for others to see.

8. Build a cabin using Lincoln Logs, twigs, Popsicle sticks, or other materials. Bring it to your classroom for others to see.

9. Get J.C. Penney, Sears, Gander Mountain, L.L. Bean, or other catalogs and magazines. Design a collage depicting fun in the country.

10. Surviving outdoors requires knowledge and skill. Invite a guest speaker to talk to your class about this. Visit an "outdoors" store and get ideas for this presentation.

Ft. Waterdale

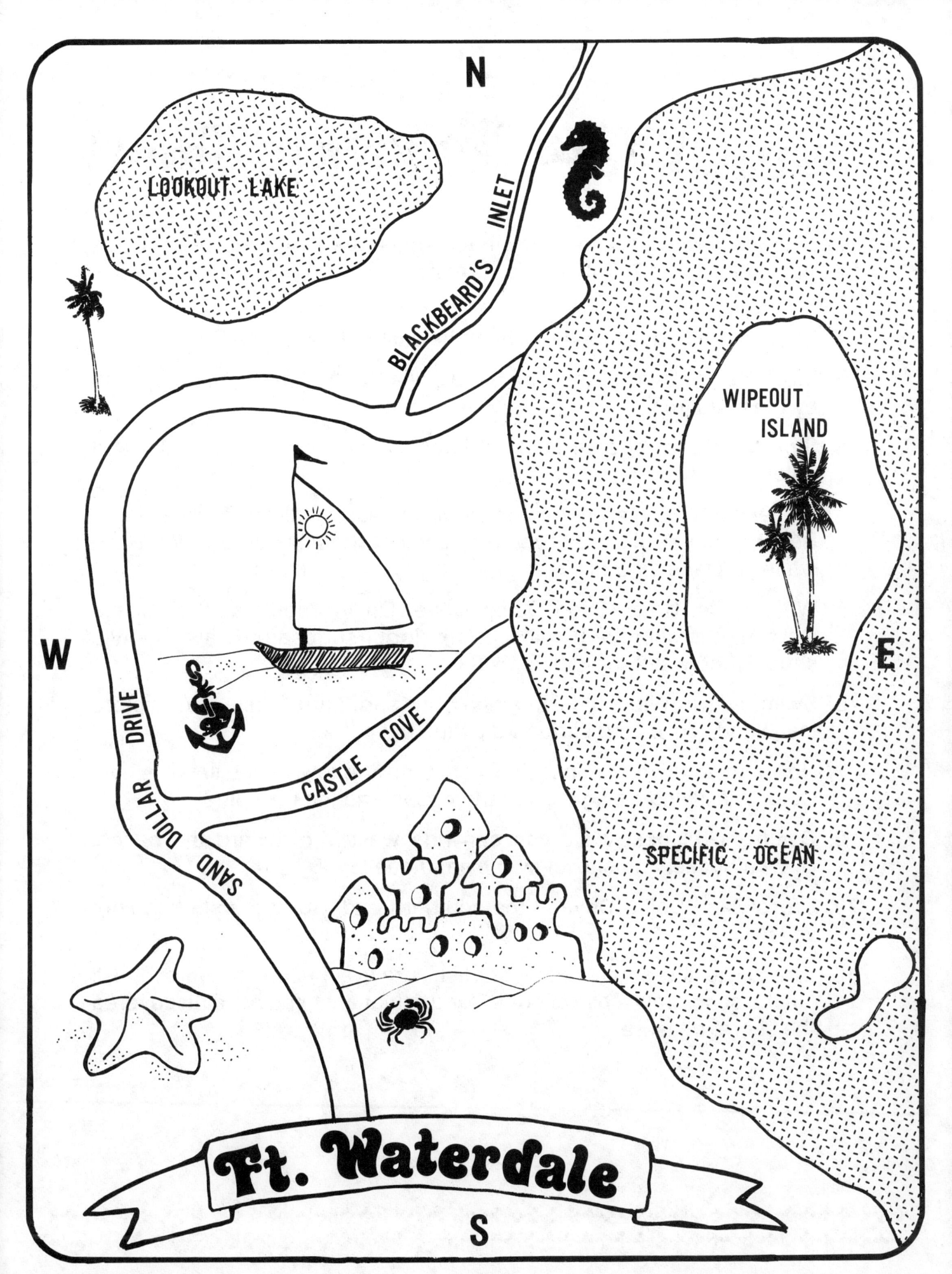

N / S / E / W

- Lookout Lake
- Blackbeard's Inlet
- Wipeout Island
- Castle Cove
- Sand Dollar Drive
- Specific Ocean

Waterdale Treasure Hunt

Many pirates were said to have buried treasures along the beach. Use the map on page 43. Follow the directions carefully to find the secret treasure.

1. Print your first name on the sail of the sailboat. Color the boat.

2. Move west. Travel north along Sand Dollar Drive. Draw yourself resting by the palm tree.

3. Stop for a boat ride on Lookout Lake. Draw a boat on the lake and color it yellow.

4. Travel east. Draw a bridge across Blackbeard's Inlet near Sea Horse Beach. Color it black. Leave your towel and backpack on the beach while you take a swim.

5. Walk south. Cross Sand Dollar Drive. On the north side of Castle Cove by the shore you will rent a colorful surfboard. Draw the little shop by the water. Color it.

6. Swim over to Wipeout Island with your surfboard. While you explore the island, leave your surfboard by the palm tree.

7. Now surf south in the Specific Ocean, moving toward the small island. Color this island orange. Color the ocean and the lake blue.

8. Catch the biggest wave you can ride westward toward the beach. Draw a bucket and shovel by the sand castle.

9. Cross Sand Dollar Drive at the southern end. Color the starfish light yellow.

10. Directly to the south of the starfish, draw a brown treasure chest. On the sand draw a pile of gold. Congratulations! You have discovered the secret treasure.

Copyright © 1990, Good Apple, Inc.

GA1145

Projects to Do
ABOUT THE BEACH

1. Have a tasting party for your class. Bring in samples of various foods found at the beach. Examples might include shrimp, clams, crabs, oysters, fish (various types), saltwater taffy, etc. Invite other students to prepare foods with you because this can be quite expensive.

2. Set up a child's large plastic swimming pool in your classroom. Fill it with sand (do this outside if possible). Design a sand castle or sand sculpture and share it with others in your school. You may want to work with a partner.

3. Swimming and suntanning at the ocean can be dangerous. Invite a lifeguard to talk to your class about safety at the beach.

4. Make a large paper doll. Design several summer outfits for your doll. Include clothes for swimming, casual, and formal wear.

5. The ocean is full of life. Make an aquarium and bring it to school for your classmates to see. Be able to tell the children about the plants and animals you have included.

6. Bring your collection of seashells to class (wrap them so they will arrive safely). Explain to your class the different types of shells and what animals used them.

7. Create objects using seashells. If you have several shells, give them to other children in your class and teach them how to make something. Have an exhibit of the projects when they are completed.

8. Select an ocean animal. Research it. Bring your report and colored drawings to class for others to see.

9. Use a large shoe box and make a diorama of an ocean scene. When all objects are inside, cover the front of the box with plastic wrap. Display your project in the classroom.

10. Make a list of several beach careers. Write a report about one that interests you (interview someone special if you like).

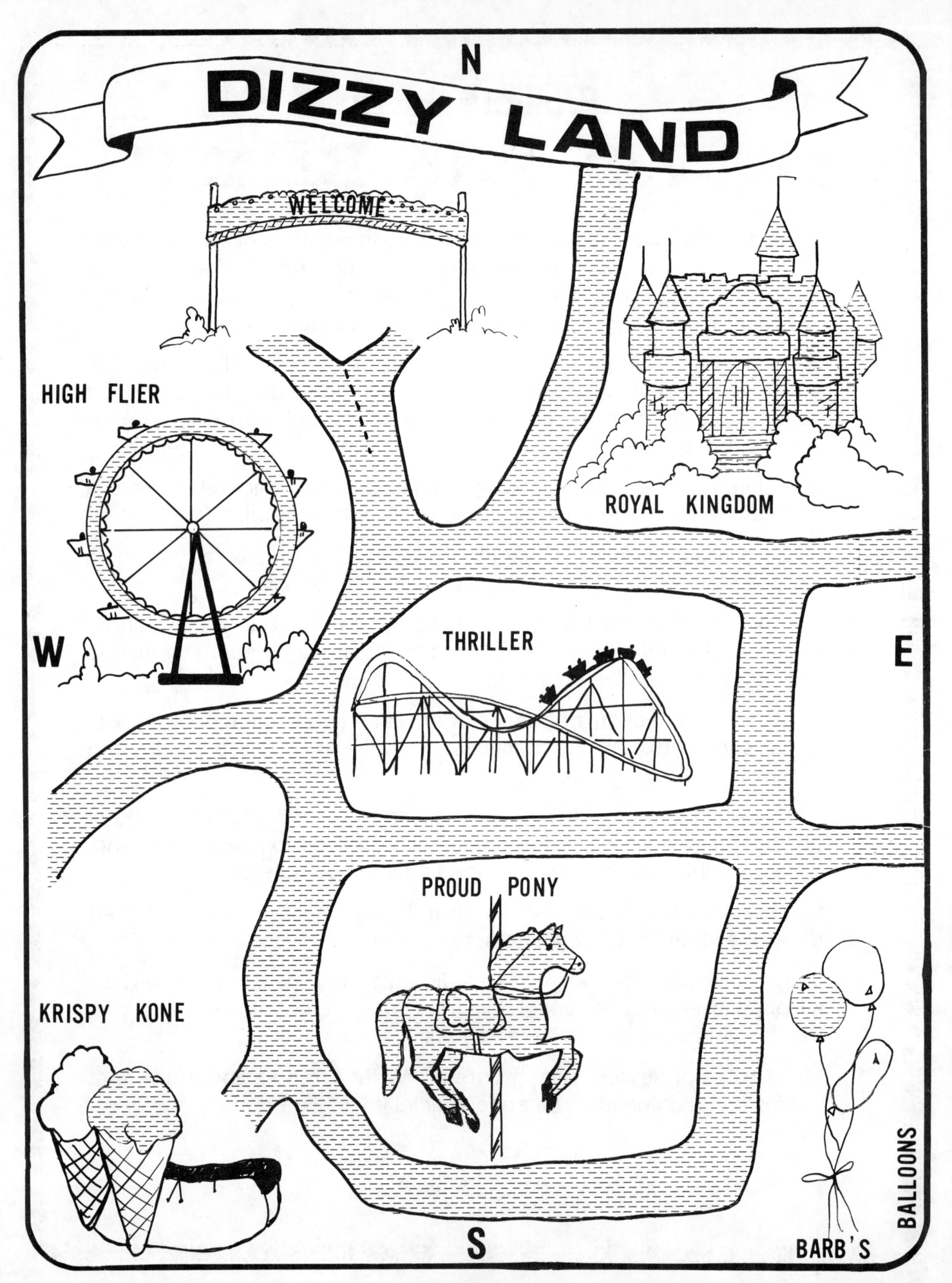

DIZZY LAND

N · W · E · S

WELCOME

HIGH FLIER

ROYAL KINGDOM

THRILLER

PROUD PONY

KRISPY KONE

BARB'S BALLOONS

ADMIT ONE
to
Dizzy Land

Your class is going to Dizzy Land for the day. Your teacher gave you this map so that you and your friends could become familiar with the park before the class trip. Can you find your way around? Let's see. Just follow the simple directions below.

1. Are you ready for the big day? Write your first and last name on your map and follow your teacher's directions. Have a great time!
2. Buy your tickets at the entrance to the park. Draw a ticket booth on the right side of the park gate as you enter from the north. Color it brown.
3. What ride is directly south of the ticket booth? _____
4. Color that ride green. Put an X on the seat you want to ride in.
5. The only bathrooms in the park are southwest of the High Flier. Draw them.
6. If you want a light lunch, stop at _____. Draw two picnic tables there where you can eat.
7. In the eastern section of Dizzy Land you will find your favorite ride. Draw it. Give it a name.
8. _____ is at the southern end of the park. Color it gold.
9. Only children ages 8 and up are allowed to go on the _____. This ride might scare younger boys and girls. Color this ride red.
10. A good place to buy souvenirs is _____. Color one red, one blue, and one yellow.
11. In the northeast corner of the park is the _____. This would be a good place to spend some time if it rains because all of the games and the entertainment are inside.
12. To the right of Proud Pony you will find a First Aid Station. Draw a white flag with a red cross in the center of it.
13. At 3:00 you and your friends will meet to the right of the welcome sign as you leave Dizzy Land. Draw yourself standing there with two friends.

Projects to Do

About the Amusement Park

1. Make a large, colorful mural of an amusement park. This can be a park you have visited or one of your own creation.

2. Most amusement parks have little booths or shops. Think of a shop you would like to operate and write a paragraph explaining why.

3. Design your own amusement park. Give your park a title. Draw a map showing the entire park or the section you like best (kiddie section, wild west, etc.).

4. Choose a famous amusement park. Collect brochures and other information about it to share with your class.

5. Design an amusement park T-shirt. Art/Fabric stores carry crayons for just this purpose!

6. Write an adventure story about an amusement park. Ideas might include "The Runaway Roller Coaster," "The Tunnel of ...," "Our Class Trip," etc.

7. Compile a list of safety tips for parents to include when they take their children to an amusement park. Add illustrations if you like.

8. Make an alphabetical list of at least twenty rides found in an amusement park. Now create a word search puzzle using this list.

9. Pretend that your class is going on a field trip to an amusement park. Write down all of the expenses they might have. Include actual prices if you can.

10. At most amusement parks, the lines for rides are usually pretty long. Think of at least ten things you could do with your friends while standing patiently in line.

TRAVEL TIPS

On Your Mark

* Spend a lot of time selecting your vacation spot. Gather information and read about it to be sure that this is the vacation of your dreams.
* Keep in mind the number of people going on the trip, their ages, the length of stay, and interesting things to do.
* Apply for a passport and get the proper vaccinations if traveling abroad.
* Begin saving your money in advance so that you can enjoy the opportunities.
* Make your airline and hotel reservations if you know your vacation dates.

Get Set

* Ask someone you trust to care for your pets, plants, house, and garden.
* Stop your mail and your newspaper if you will be away longer than a few days.
* Refill prescriptions and take the necessary medication with you. Take along the phone numbers of your doctors.
* Buy proper clothing and a good pair of shoes!
* Buy a good camera and try it before your vacation. Turn your batteries around in your camera while en route so that they won't cause problems in your camera.
* Give your trip itinerary to a relative or friend so that he/she can reach you if necessary.
* Pack a small, nylon, fold-up travel bag in your suitcase to use during day trips or for souvenirs.
* Keep a small, hand-held bag with you for medication, maps, travel information, cameras, and a change of clothes in case your luggage gets lost en route.
* Decide which clothes you will need. Wash them and pack them early in a sturdy suitcase with your name and address on it.
* Get traveler's checks (and foreign currency) if needed.
* Get a good night's sleep before you go.

GO

Our Hotel features:

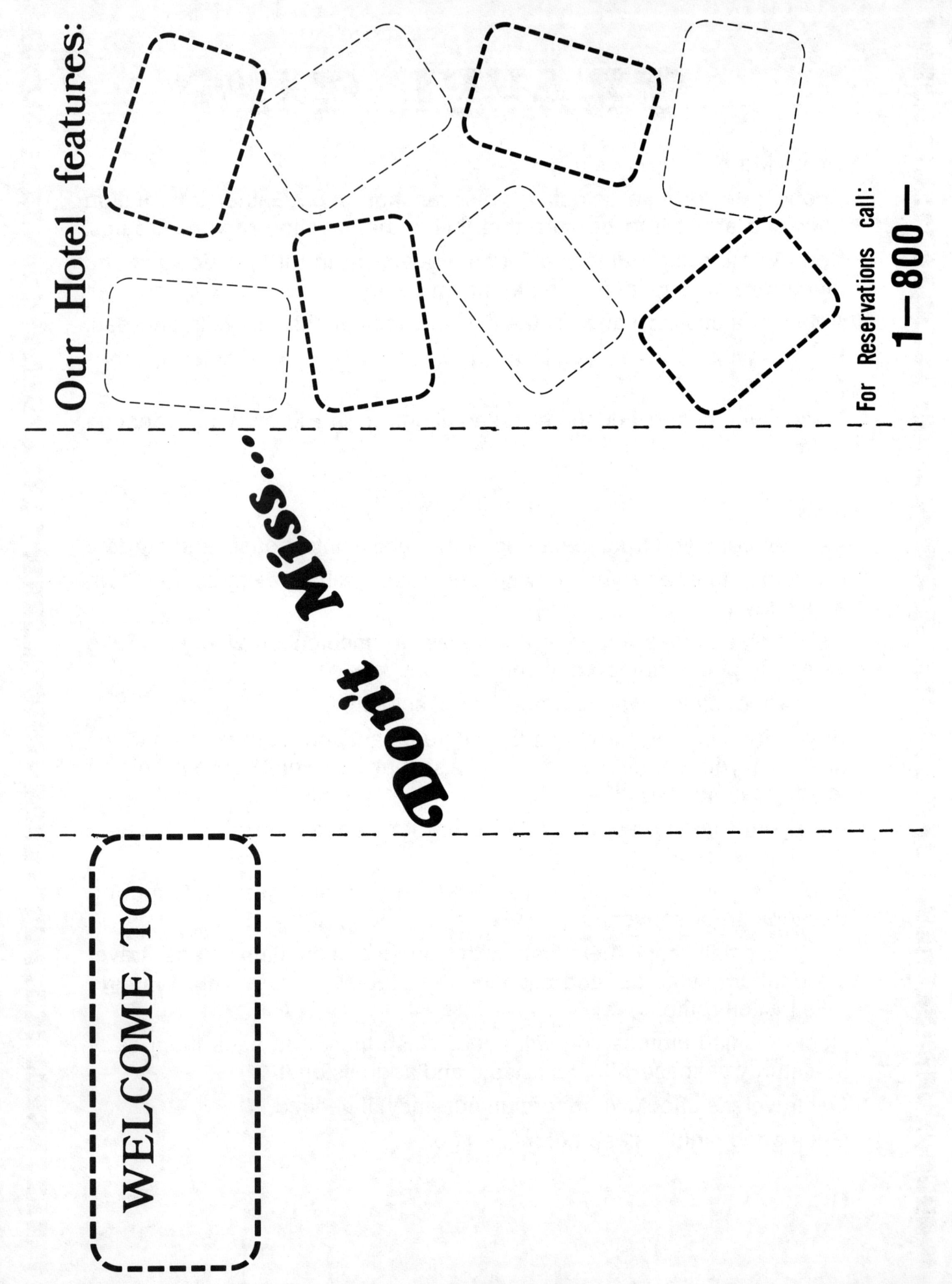

For Reservations call:
1—800—

Don't Miss...

WELCOME TO

VACATION PLANNER

ITINERARY | EXPENSES

Travel

Lodging

Food

Entertainment

Tips

Souvenirs

TUNE UP

To keep your engine running smoothly,
  Give it proper care,
Lubricate those moving parts—
  Watch out! There are none to spare.
Balance it with work and play
  So it can operate—
Don't wait until it gets real old—
  By then it's just too late!
Grind the rough spots, polish it,
  And watch the shine come through—
Tune it up the best you can;
  It'll run as good as new.
Now take it for a road test,
  Challenge it in every way—
Don't let your engine idle
  Or it'll waste away!

TUNE UP YOUR BODY

Here are several ways to keep your children entertained and physically fit this summer! Little or no equipment is required.

Treasure Hunts:
Place notes in sequence around the house which require children to hop three times, skip around the room, bounce a ball, jog in place, and touch their toes. Reward them with a trip to the park, time outside in the sandbox, etc.

Hula Hoops:
Great for coordination! Use them to rotate around the body; roll them with your hand; jump them like a rope; lay them on the ground and jump into them.

Beanbags:
Great for entertainment during parties! Hide them; toss them into a clothes basket; catch them; play hot potato with music (like musical chairs).

Ropes:
Alone or with a friend, they're fun to use! Jump them; swing one end and let children hop over them; twirl them like lassos and create interesting routines to music (scarves or streamers can also be used in this way).

Balls:
Create several activities of your own using various sizes and types of balls: Nerf, Ping-Pong, racquetballs, tennis balls, basketballs, soft rubber balls, soccer balls, volleyballs, and croquet balls. Try throwing, catching, bouncing, spinning, balancing, and hitting them.

Old-Fashioned Games:
1. Hopscotch (Indoors draw hopscotch on a vinyl shower curtain and tape it to the floor.)
2. Jacks (Teach various styles.)

Parachute:
Involve all the children for this great activity! With all of the children holding the edge of the parachute, try the following: walk left; walk right; hold high and circle around; hold at waist and circle; high/low motion quickly; all hide under while holding parachute down to the ground; wave motion which rotates around; one side high, other side low; bounce balls or light object on it.

Lummi Sticks:
Cut an old broom handle into 12-14 inch lengths. Have children grasp the sticks in the center and touch the ends to the ground, click the sticks together, flip the sticks, pass them to a partner beside them, and toss them to an opposite partner. Add music and create a routine.

With Music:
Try aerobics, always gradually increasing endurance and exercises.
Bounce balls, twirl ropes/ribbons.
Choreograph dances alone or with friends (try pole dancing).
Create hula hoop routines.
Play march records and lead friends in various formations, stressing right, left, right, left movement.
Practice baton twirling.

In Confined Areas:
Stretch in place; roll eyes; rotate body, place head between legs; shake arms, legs, fingers; wiggle body parts; roll head slowly in a circle. Try the Hokey-Pokey or Simon Says. Kids will love it!

TUNE UP YOUR MIND

* Many children don't know their math facts.
* Many children memorize the facts in order and cannot answer specific facts with speed and accuracy.
* Several techniques can be tried to teach math facts.
* Children need regular reinforcement to maintain math skills (older children especially need speed drills).
* Some children will never learn math facts and must be taught other ways to function when all techniques tried are unsuccessful.

Teaching suggestions for parents and teachers:
1. Write a troublesome fact on the bathroom or hallway mirror.
2. Make or buy math flash cards. Place the cards in a Baggie. Review the facts the student already knows frequently, and work one at a time on a few specific facts that the child finds difficult to learn.
3. Write a troublesome fact/facts on the refrigerator.
4. Teach a fact a day. Every time you think of it, ask the child that particular fact (when he lines up, when he is watching TV, etc.).
5. Design a board game and use the flash cards as game cards.
6. Play fact bingo. Record facts and answers in the boxes.
7. Write a troublesome fact on the child's napkin in his lunch box.
8. Play math facts records (available at educational supply stores).
9. Use incentive charts.
10. Try the buddy system for studying.
11. Use a fact work sheet for different purposes (accuracy or speed).
12. Study one set of math facts at a time.
13. Teach facts using math pairs: $3 \times 6 = 18$, $6 \times 3 = 18$.
14. Create a math facts number search (like the word search but use numbers).
15. Use magic slates that erase when the cover is lifted (great to use when traveling).
16. Buy a small chalkboard (lap size) and use old socks as erasers.
17. Use a calculator or facts chart when all else fails.

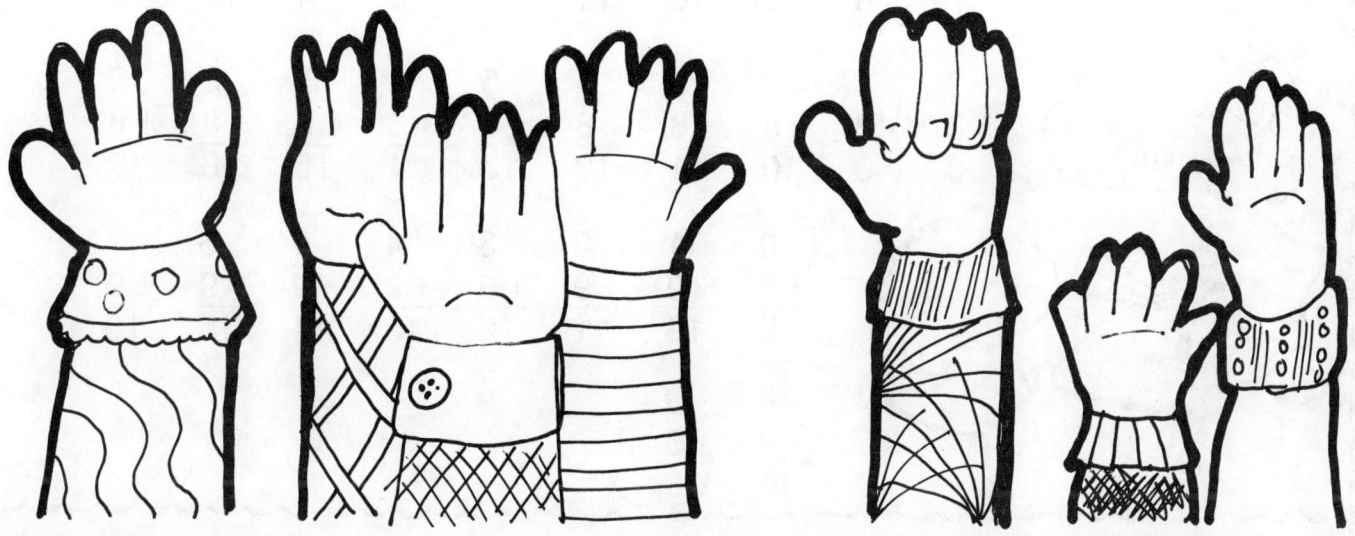

Addition Facts

0 +0 ― 0	1 +0 ― 1	2 +0 ― 2	3 +0 ― 3	4 +0 ― 4	5 +0 ― 5	6 +0 ― 6	7 +0 ― 7	8 +0 ― 8	9 +0 ― 9
0 +1 ― 1	1 +1 ― 2	2 +1 ― 3	3 +1 ― 4	4 +1 ― 5	5 +1 ― 6	6 +1 ― 7	7 +1 ― 8	8 +1 ― 9	9 +1 ― 10
0 +2 ― 2	1 +2 ― 3	2 +2 ― 4	3 +2 ― 5	4 +2 ― 6	5 +2 ― 7	6 +2 ― 8	7 +2 ― 9	8 +2 ― 10	9 +2 ― 11
0 +3 ― 3	1 +3 ― 4	2 +3 ― 5	3 +3 ― 6	4 +3 ― 7	5 +3 ― 8	6 +3 ― 9	7 +3 ― 10	8 +3 ― 11	9 +3 ― 12
0 +4 ― 4	1 +4 ― 5	2 +4 ― 6	3 +4 ― 7	4 +4 ― 8	5 +4 ― 9	6 +4 ― 10	7 +4 ― 11	8 +4 ― 12	9 +4 ― 13
0 +5 ― 5	1 +5 ― 6	2 +5 ― 7	3 +5 ― 8	4 +5 ― 9	5 +5 ― 10	6 +5 ― 11	7 +5 ― 12	8 +5 ― 13	9 +5 ― 14
0 +6 ― 6	1 +6 ― 7	2 +6 ― 8	3 +6 ― 9	4 +6 ― 10	5 +6 ― 11	6 +6 ― 12	7 +6 ― 13	8 +6 ― 14	9 +6 ― 15

0 +7 ― 7	1 +7 ― 8	2 +7 ― 9	3 +7 ― 10	4 +7 ― 11	5 +7 ― 12	6 +7 ― 13	7 +7 ― 14	8 +7 ― 15	9 +7 ― 16
0 +8 ― 8	1 +8 ― 9	2 +8 ― 10	3 +8 ― 11	4 +8 ― 12	5 +8 ― 13	6 +8 ― 14	7 +8 ― 15	8 +8 ― 16	9 +8 ― 17

0 +9 ― 9	1 +9 ― 10	2 +9 ― 11	3 +9 ― 12	4 +9 ― 13	5 +9 ― 14	6 +9 ― 15	7 +9 ― 16

8 +9 ― 17	9 +9 ― 18

Yum!

I love MATH!

SUBTRACTION FACTS

0 −0 ─ 0	1 −0 ─ 1	2 −0 ─ 2	3 −0 ─ 3	4 −0 ─ 4	5 −0 ─ 5	6 −0 ─ 6	7 −0 ─ 7	8 −0 ─ 8	9 −0 ─ 9
1 −1 ─ 0	2 −1 ─ 1	3 −1 ─ 2	4 −1 ─ 3	5 −1 ─ 4	6 −1 ─ 5	7 −1 ─ 6	8 −1 ─ 7	9 −1 ─ 8	10 −1 ─ 9
2 −2 ─ 0	3 −2 ─ 1	4 −2 ─ 2	5 −2 ─ 3	6 −2 ─ 4	7 −2 ─ 5	8 −2 ─ 6	9 −2 ─ 7	10 −2 ─ 8	11 −2 ─ 9
3 −3 ─ 0	4 −3 ─ 1	5 −3 ─ 2	6 −3 ─ 3	7 −3 ─ 4	8 −3 ─ 5	9 −3 ─ 6	10 −3 ─ 7	11 −3 ─ 8	12 −3 ─ 9
4 −4 ─ 0	5 −4 ─ 1	6 −4 ─ 2	7 −4 ─ 3	8 −4 ─ 4	9 −4 ─ 5	10 −4 ─ 6	11 −4 ─ 7	12 −4 ─ 8	13 −4 ─ 9
5 −5 ─ 0	6 −5 ─ 1	7 −5 ─ 2	8 −5 ─ 3	9 −5 ─ 4	10 −5 ─ 5	11 −5 ─ 6	12 −5 ─ 7	13 −5 ─ 8	14 −5 ─ 9
6 −6 ─ 0	7 −6 ─ 1	8 −6 ─ 2	9 −6 ─ 3	10 −6 ─ 4	11 −6 ─ 5	12 −6 ─ 6	13 −6 ─ 7	14 −6 ─ 8	15 −6 ─ 9
7 −7 ─ 0	8 −7 ─ 1	9 −7 ─ 2	10 −7 ─ 3	11 −7 ─ 4	12 −7 ─ 5	13 −7 ─ 6	14 −7 ─ 7	15 −7 ─ 8	16 −7 ─ 9
8 −8 ─ 0	9 −8 ─ 1	10 −8 ─ 2	11 −8 ─ 3	12 −8 ─ 4	13 −8 ─ 5	14 −8 ─ 6	15 −8 ─ 7	16 −8 ─ 8	17 −8 ─ 9
9 −9 ─ 0	10 −9 ─ 1	11 −9 ─ 2	12 −9 ─ 3	13 −9 ─ 4	14 −9 ─ 5	15 −9 ─ 6	16 −9 ─ 7	17 −9 ─ 8	18 −9 ─ 9

9 − 5 =

Let me think....

Copyright © 1990, Good Apple, Inc.

GA1145

Multiplication Facts

0 × 0 = 0	1 × 0 = 0	2 × 0 = 0	3 × 0 = 0
0 × 1 = 0	1 × 1 = 1	2 × 1 = 2	3 × 1 = 3
0 × 2 = 0	1 × 2 = 2	2 × 2 = 4	3 × 2 = 6
0 × 3 = 0	1 × 3 = 3	2 × 3 = 6	3 × 3 = 9
0 × 4 = 0	1 × 4 = 4	2 × 4 = 8	3 × 4 = 12
0 × 5 = 0	1 × 5 = 5	2 × 5 = 10	3 × 5 = 15
0 × 6 = 0	1 × 6 = 6	2 × 6 = 12	3 × 6 = 18
0 × 7 = 0	1 × 7 = 7	2 × 7 = 14	3 × 7 = 21
0 × 8 = 0	1 × 8 = 8	2 × 8 = 16	3 × 8 = 24
0 × 9 = 0	1 × 9 = 9	2 × 9 = 18	3 × 9 = 27
0 × 10 = 0	1 × 10 = 10	2 × 10 = 20	3 × 10 = 30
0 × 11 = 0	1 × 11 = 11	2 × 11 = 22	3 × 11 = 33
0 × 12 = 0	1 × 12 = 12	2 × 12 = 24	3 × 12 = 36

4 × 0 = 0	5 × 0 = 0	6 × 0 = 0	7 × 0 = 0
4 × 1 = 4	5 × 1 = 5	6 × 1 = 6	7 × 1 = 7
4 × 2 = 8	5 × 2 = 10	6 × 2 = 12	7 × 2 = 14
4 × 3 = 12	5 × 3 = 15	6 × 3 = 18	7 × 3 = 21
4 × 4 = 16	5 × 4 = 20	6 × 4 = 24	7 × 4 = 28
4 × 5 = 20	5 × 5 = 25	6 × 5 = 30	7 × 5 = 35
4 × 6 = 24	5 × 6 = 30	6 × 6 = 36	7 × 6 = 42
4 × 7 = 28	5 × 7 = 35	6 × 7 = 42	7 × 7 = 49
4 × 8 = 32	5 × 8 = 40	6 × 8 = 48	7 × 8 = 56
4 × 9 = 36	5 × 9 = 45	6 × 9 = 54	7 × 9 = 63
4 × 10 = 40	5 × 10 = 50	6 × 10 = 60	7 × 10 = 70
4 × 11 = 44	5 × 11 = 55	6 × 11 = 66	7 × 11 = 77
4 × 12 = 48	5 × 12 = 60	6 × 12 = 72	7 × 12 = 84

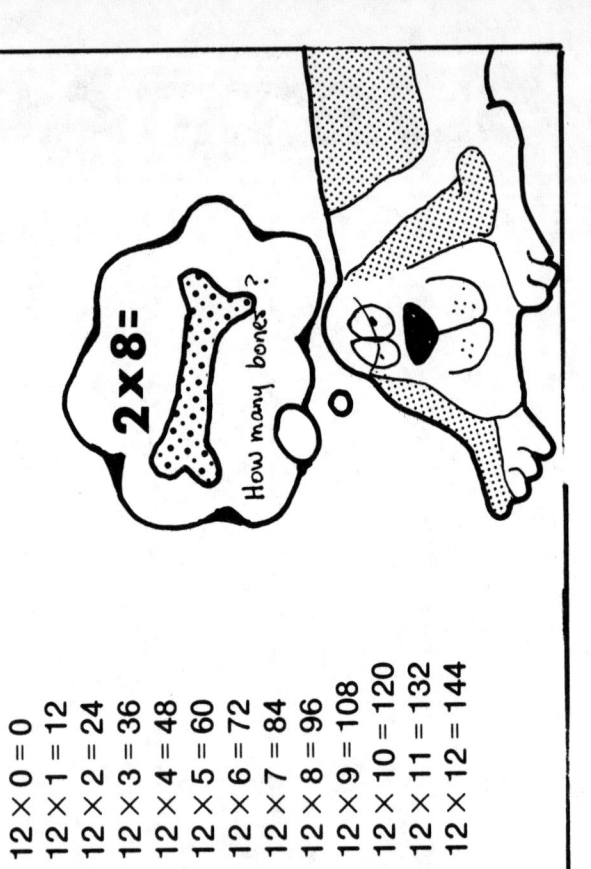

8 × 0 = 0	9 × 0 = 0	10 × 0 = 0	
8 × 1 = 8	9 × 1 = 9	10 × 1 = 10	
8 × 2 = 16	9 × 2 = 18	10 × 2 = 20	
8 × 3 = 24	9 × 3 = 27	10 × 3 = 30	
8 × 4 = 32	9 × 4 = 36	10 × 4 = 40	
8 × 5 = 40	9 × 5 = 45	10 × 5 = 50	
8 × 6 = 48	9 × 6 = 54	10 × 6 = 60	
8 × 7 = 56	9 × 7 = 63	10 × 7 = 70	
8 × 8 = 64	9 × 8 = 72	10 × 8 = 80	
8 × 9 = 72	9 × 9 = 81	10 × 9 = 90	
8 × 10 = 80	9 × 10 = 90	10 × 10 = 100	
8 × 11 = 88	9 × 11 = 99	10 × 11 = 110	
8 × 12 = 96	9 × 12 = 108	10 × 12 = 120	

11 × 0 = 0	12 × 0 = 0
11 × 1 = 11	12 × 1 = 12
11 × 2 = 22	12 × 2 = 24
11 × 3 = 33	12 × 3 = 36
11 × 4 = 44	12 × 4 = 48
11 × 5 = 55	12 × 5 = 60
11 × 6 = 66	12 × 6 = 72
11 × 7 = 77	12 × 7 = 84
11 × 8 = 88	12 × 8 = 96
11 × 9 = 99	12 × 9 = 108
11 × 10 = 110	12 × 10 = 120
11 × 11 = 121	12 × 11 = 132
11 × 12 = 132	12 × 12 = 144

2 × 8 = How many bones?

Copyright © 1990, Good Apple, Inc.

GA1145

DIVISION FACTS

$$1\overline{)1}^{\,1} \quad 1\overline{)2}^{\,2} \quad 1\overline{)3}^{\,3} \quad 1\overline{)4}^{\,4} \quad 1\overline{)5}^{\,5} \quad 1\overline{)6}^{\,6} \quad 1\overline{)7}^{\,7} \quad 1\overline{)8}^{\,8} \quad 1\overline{)9}^{\,9}$$

$$2\overline{)2}^{\,1} \quad 2\overline{)4}^{\,2} \quad 2\overline{)6}^{\,3} \quad 2\overline{)8}^{\,4} \quad 2\overline{)10}^{\,5} \quad 2\overline{)12}^{\,6} \quad 2\overline{)14}^{\,7} \quad 2\overline{)16}^{\,8} \quad 2\overline{)18}^{\,9}$$

$$3\overline{)3}^{\,1} \quad 3\overline{)6}^{\,2} \quad 3\overline{)9}^{\,3} \quad 3\overline{)12}^{\,4} \quad 3\overline{)15}^{\,5} \quad 3\overline{)18}^{\,6} \quad 3\overline{)21}^{\,7} \quad 3\overline{)24}^{\,8} \quad 3\overline{)27}^{\,9}$$

$$4\overline{)4}^{\,1} \quad 4\overline{)8}^{\,2} \quad 4\overline{)12}^{\,3} \quad 4\overline{)16}^{\,4} \quad 4\overline{)20}^{\,5} \quad 4\overline{)24}^{\,6} \quad 4\overline{)28}^{\,7} \quad 4\overline{)32}^{\,8} \quad 4\overline{)36}^{\,9}$$

$$5\overline{)5}^{\,1} \quad 5\overline{)10}^{\,2} \quad 5\overline{)15}^{\,3} \quad 5\overline{)20}^{\,4} \quad 5\overline{)25}^{\,5} \quad 5\overline{)30}^{\,6} \quad 5\overline{)35}^{\,7} \quad 5\overline{)40}^{\,8} \quad 5\overline{)45}^{\,9}$$

$$6\overline{)6}^{\,1} \quad 6\overline{)12}^{\,2} \quad 6\overline{)18}^{\,3} \quad 6\overline{)24}^{\,4} \quad 6\overline{)30}^{\,5} \quad 6\overline{)36}^{\,6} \quad 6\overline{)42}^{\,7} \quad 6\overline{)48}^{\,8} \quad 6\overline{)54}^{\,9}$$

$$7\overline{)7}^{\,1} \quad 7\overline{)14}^{\,2} \quad 7\overline{)21}^{\,3} \quad 7\overline{)28}^{\,4} \quad 7\overline{)35}^{\,5} \quad 7\overline{)42}^{\,6} \quad 7\overline{)49}^{\,7} \quad 7\overline{)56}^{\,8} \quad 7\overline{)63}^{\,9}$$

$$8\overline{)8}^{\,1} \quad 8\overline{)16}^{\,2} \quad 8\overline{)24}^{\,3} \quad 8\overline{)32}^{\,4} \quad 8\overline{)40}^{\,5} \quad 8\overline{)48}^{\,6} \quad 8\overline{)56}^{\,7} \quad 8\overline{)64}^{\,8} \quad 8\overline{)72}^{\,9}$$

$$9\overline{)9}^{\,1} \quad 9\overline{)18}^{\,2} \quad 9\overline{)27}^{\,3} \quad 9\overline{)36}^{\,4} \quad 9\overline{)45}^{\,5} \quad 9\overline{)54}^{\,6} \quad 9\overline{)63}^{\,7} \quad 9\overline{)72}^{\,8} \quad 9\overline{)81}^{\,9}$$

6 ÷ 3 =

Ugh! Ugh!

PIT STOP

A picnic just in time for spring! Grill a footlong hot dog story, toss in a tasty choice of story elements, try a few story quenchers, examine a few basket case mysteries, add a ripe bunch of story starters, and sweeten the lunch with a few fantasies. Your children will be excited about this special creative writing center.

The student contract will provide an efficient way to keep track of each child's progress. As each section of the station is completed, color in the corresponding area on the contract page. You will need to determine specifically your method of grading and length of time you wish to designate for this station. There are six different types of writing assignments. Slight teacher preparation is required if you use these ideas as a station. Alter the activities to satisfy the needs of your own classroom.

Once the station is ready, decide whether you want children to be scheduled through the activities or to go freely to complete story assignments.

If you choose not to use the station as planned, try introducing a particular type of story to the class and use the ideas provided as suggested, creating background for certain types of writing activities to be completed as a class.

PACK·A·LUNCH

WRITING CENTER

This creative writing center is sure to delight your students. Set up a display in a quiet spot in your room where children can work with the folder activities independently after instructions from you. Duplicate a student contract for each child. As students complete each section, remind them to color in that part of the contract and place the work in the folder for you to check. When all sections of the contract are completed, the "lunch is packed." Supplement station activities when/if the need arises.

TIPS:
1. Keep your work neat.
2. Respect station materials and area.
3. Label your work.
4. Place finished work in proper place.

Station Folders

Finished Work

Student Contracts

Pencils

Copyright © 1990, Good Apple, Inc.

GA1145

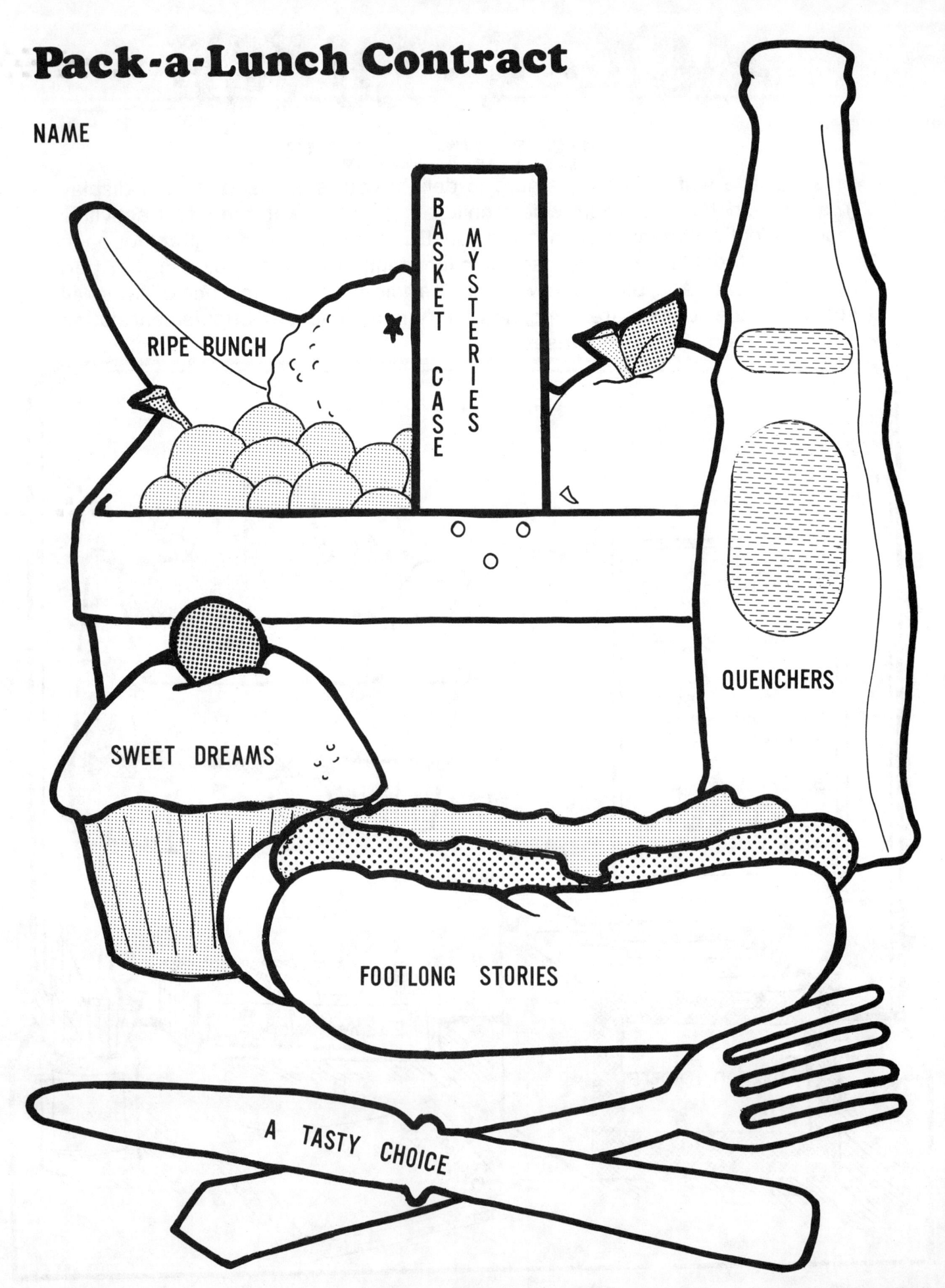

Pack-a-Lunch Contract

NAME

RIPE BUNCH

BASKET CASE MYSTERIES

QUENCHERS

SWEET DREAMS

FOOTLONG STORIES

A TASTY CHOICE

Place the label below on the cover of a file folder. Cut out several grape patterns made from oaktag (see page 65). Place them in a pocket on the inside of the folder. On the opposite inside section of the folder, staple the story starter ideas. Above the grape patterns write these simple directions:

1. Write your name and the date on your pattern.
2. Choose a story starter idea from the folder.
3. Copy the starter onto your pattern neatly and add your own ending. Be sure to indent.
4. Place completed work in your folder and lay it in the box at the station.
5. Return all materials to their places.

THE RIPE BUNCH

The Ripe Bunch of Story Starters

1. One stormy night my friend and I decided to go for a walk. Wearing raincoats, we slipped out the back door and followed the flashlight's beam. As we rounded the corner of the house . . .

2. Last night I couldn't get to sleep. My whole family had gone to bed early. I stayed up to watch a scary movie. During the commercial, I fixed myself a snack and returned to the living room to watch the ending of the movie. Just then . . .

3. Mom said I could have a party for my 10th birthday. I was so excited I thought the day would never come. Finally, my birthday arrived and I . . .

4. Last summer my family decided to go camping. We packed the gear in the jeep and off we went. Dad . . .

5. The tapping grew louder and louder. I sat up in bed. The noise seemed to be coming from my bedroom window. I followed the sound. Just as I reached the window I saw . . .

6. "You've won! You've won!" shouted the announcer. He came toward me with the tickets. I couldn't believe my eyes. His voice echoed with excitement. He told me . . .

7. I had the best surprise of all. Yesterday Dad came home with a . . .

8. My family had the neatest vacation last summer. We went to . . .

9. "Let's go in," said Monica. "There is a large room and it looks pretty light inside. If we all stay together . . ."

THE RIPE BUNCH OF STORY STARTERS

Glue the label below to the cover of a file folder. Duplicate a few pages of the cupcake pattern onto oaktag (see page 68). Cut out the fantasy writing ideas and glue each one to a cupcake. Place oaktag cupcakes in a pocket on the inside of the folder.

Make three small clouds to place above the pocket stating the three elements that can make a story a fantasy: 1) characters 2) setting 3) plot.

Now write these simple instructions for writing a fantasy on the other inside section of the folder.

1. Write your heading on your paper.
2. Choose a cupcake. Write the story beginning on your paper and add your ending to complete your fantasy.
3. Place your work in your folder and leave it at the station.

SWEET DREAMS

Copyright © 1990, Good Apple, Inc.

GA1145

SWEET DREAMS

There was once a very poor boy. Children teased him because he had no bicycle. One Christmas his dream came true. Under the tree stood a bicycle—but this one was different. It could . . .

In an old, crooked tree there lived a creature. It resembled a bird, but it made sounds like a dog. The creature . . .

I was walking to school one day when I noticed that the school bus beside me sputtered a little as it passed. I hadn't gone far when I realized the bus began to fly. I . . .

Teresa and I were sitting on the beach watching waves gently splash our feet. When the water settled in the sand, a little man appeared, staring at us with a puzzled look. He . . .

The rocket neared the planet with full throttle. After circling it a few times, the astronaut eased the spaceship to a smooth landing. When he opened the hatch, he noticed the planet was bright and covered with tall, round . . .

One of the boys in band class invited me to spend the weekend at his house. His mom picked us up and headed home. She drove the car to the edge of the bay, where she stopped. She pushed a button. The car drifted into the water where it became a submarine. We . . .

Last October Mom asked me to sweep the porch. I picked up the broom and began to clean when the broom . . .

My friends and I had a sleepover at my house. Dad let us stay up late to watch TV. After my family had gone to bed, strange noises sounded on the . . .

Jeremy was playing in Dad's workshop, tinkering with the tools. He did this often and seemed to create the wildest things. Tonight he built . . .

We packed the car and headed for the vacation of our dreams. After driving all night, we arrived at the condo to find . . .

SWEET DREAMS

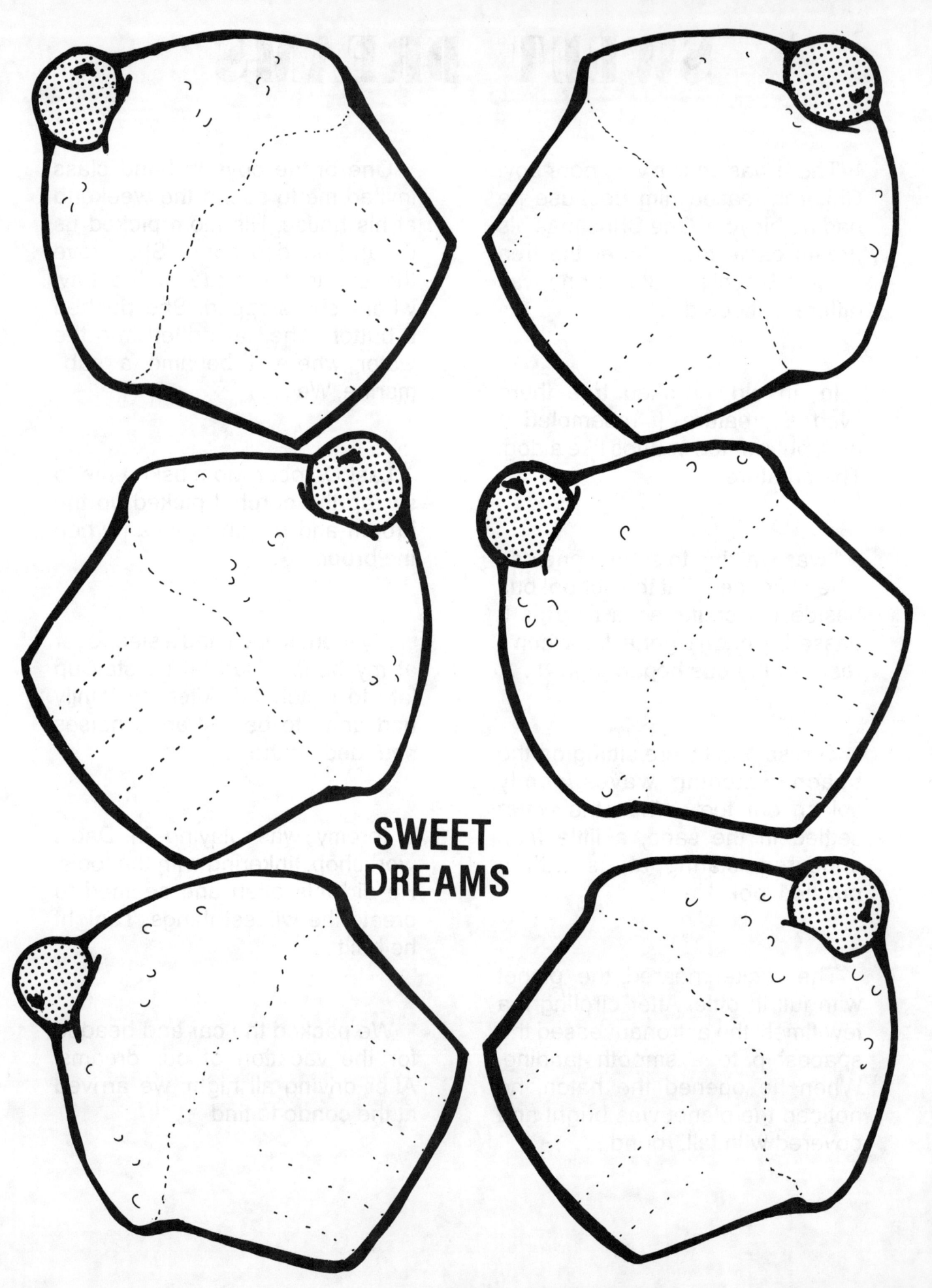

On the outside of a folder glue the label below. Make a few oaktag copies of the magnifying glass page (see page 71). Cut out the "clues" and glue them to the center of each magnifying glass. Place cut out magnifying glasses into a pocket inside the folder. On the opposite inside section of the folder, write these directions for completing this activity.

1. Write the heading on your paper.
2. Choose a magnifying glass containing story clues.
3. Use the clues with some of your own to complete a mystery story.
4. Give your story a title. Place it in your folder and leave it at the station.

BASKET CASE MYSTERIES

Copyright © 1990, Good Apple, Inc.

GA1145

Basket Case Mysteries

shovel
fresh dirt
treasure box
footprints
gold coins

small boat
empty oxygen tank
broken swim mask
black wet suit
ocean floor

rocket
journal
darkness
eager astronauts
experiments

map
new rig
missing driver
broken C.B.
open cab

crowds
New York City
speeding elevators
people hurrying
skyscrapers

footsteps
darkroom
open window
cut telephone line
telephone

castle
steep cliff
powerful king
knights on horseback
crowded dungeon
peasants

blackness
clammy feeling
stalagmites/stalactites
flashlight beam
water dripping
bats zooming

sad eyes
red nose
polka-dot costume
bright balloons
circus tents

airport
large jet
hidden camera
newspaper
suitcase
passport

Basket Case Mysteries

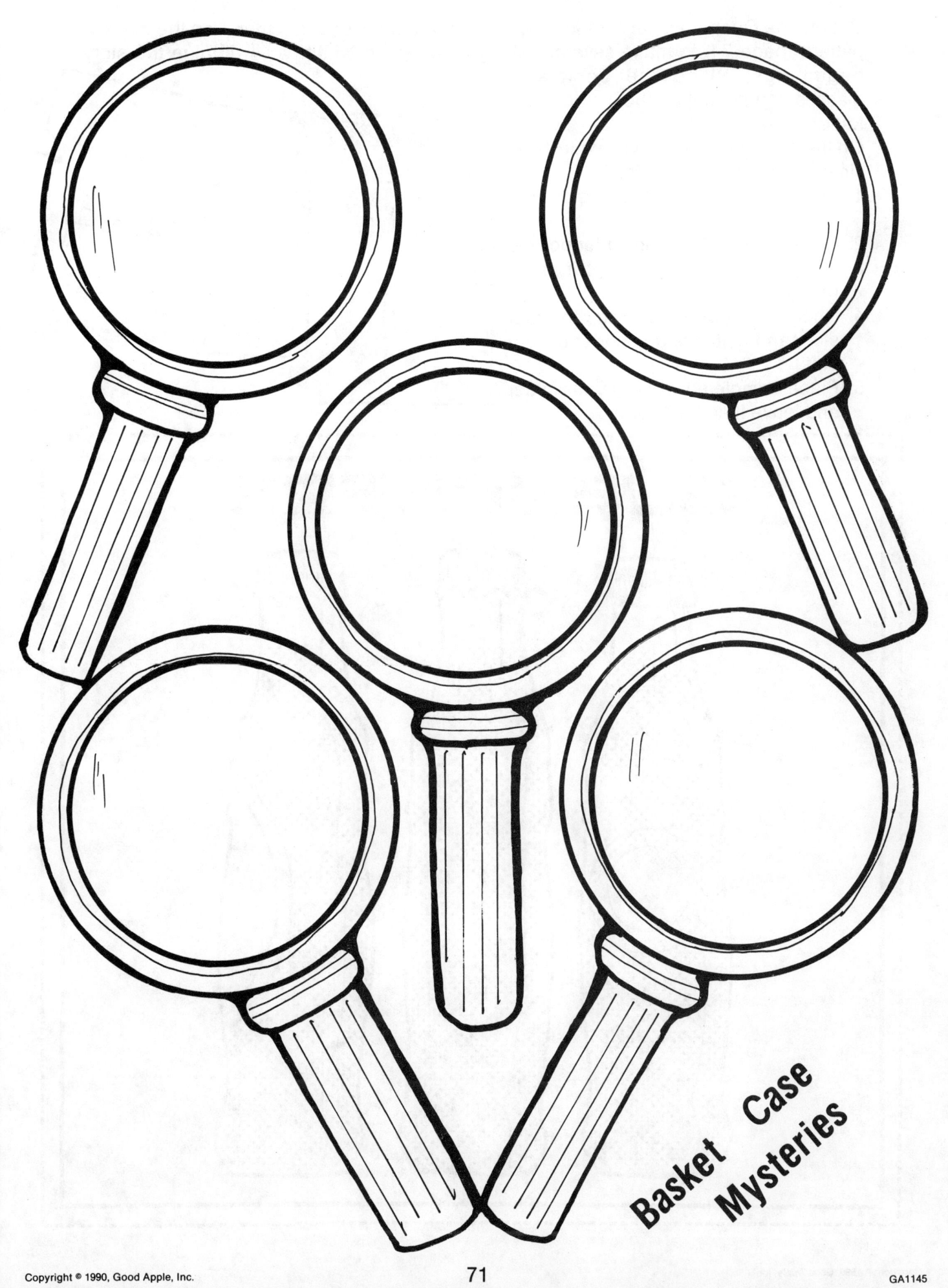

Cut out the Quenchers label below and glue it to the cover of a folder. Use the glasses pattern (page 74) to make several oaktag patterns on which you will glue the story beginnings. Place the completed glasses in a pocket on the inside of the folder.

On the opposite inside cover, write these simple directions for students:
1. Write your name and the date on your paper.
2. Select a glass from the folder pocket.
3. Copy the Quencher onto your paper neatly.
4. Choose one of the endings for your story and write the remainder of your plot.
5. Place completed work in your folder and leave it at the station.

QUENCHERS

Copyright © 1990, Good Apple, Inc.

GA1145

QUENCHERS

Ron and I rented a yellow boat with a bright sail. We put our equipment on board and set sail. It took us awhile to reach deep water. By noon the cool breeze reminded us that summer was our favorite time to sail. We lay gazing at the blue sky. Suddenly, just ahead, there appeared: An island—A shark.

The spaceship sped through the darkness. The controls were blinking, signaling an object ahead. Brighter and brighter the lights flashed. The astronauts decided to: Return to Earth—Explore the new planet.

One day last spring we went backpacking. After hiking all day we still hadn't reached camp where our leaders were waiting for us. Tired and hungry, we rounded the hill to discover: A bear—A snake.

Last Saturday night I was baby-sitting. Two-year-old Ann would not stop crying. I rocked her to sleep and lay her in her bed. As I came back into the living room I heard a knock on the window. I: Looked outside—Called for help.

My cousin and I were playing in the barn. I threw a handful of hay on Aaron, only to discover a mouse pawing my hand, trying to escape. I: Decided to keep the mouse as a pet—Let the mouse go.

My friends and I went to an amusement park. Soon after we arrived, I got separated from the group. I: Tried to find my friends—Rode by myself.

I entered a contest and won. For my prize I: Got $200,000 a year for the rest of my life—Got $10,000,000 in cash at once.

While on a safari in Africa, I discovered a wounded leopard. I nursed him for a few days and then decided to: Leave him in Africa—Take him to a zoo.

QUENCHER

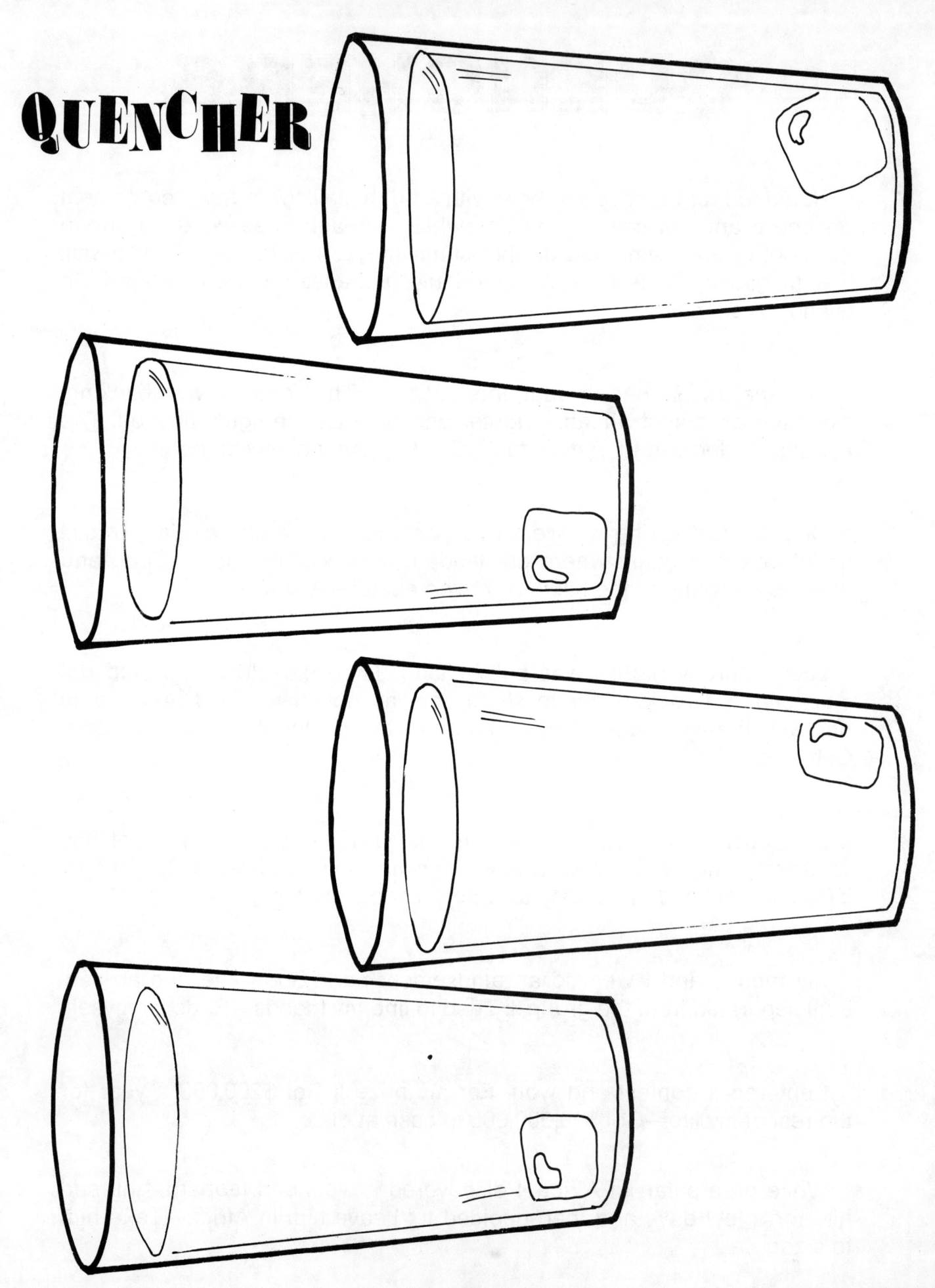

Paste the label below on the front of a folder. Use the hot dog pattern provided (see page 77) and make several footlong oaktag hot dogs. Duplicate several word banks to glue to the backs of the hot dogs.

Place the hot dogs in a pocket on the inside of the folder.

Write these simple directions for students on the opposite inside cover of the folder:

1. Choose one hot dog from the folder.
2. Write your name on it.
3. Use the word bank plus words of your own to write a story. Give it a title.
4. Place finished work in your folder at the center.

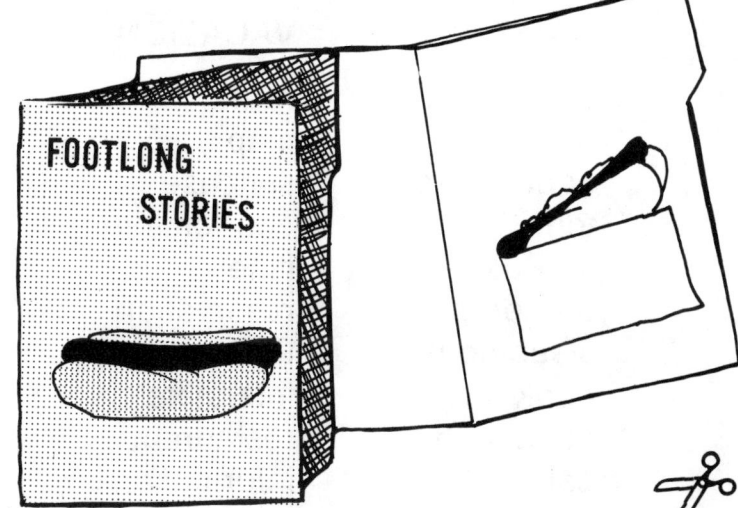

FOOTLONG STORIES

Footlong Stories

CAMP	VACATION	FAMILY	SUMMER
campfire	route	reunion	bike
swimming pool	map	brother	swim
counselors	suitcase	sister	play
tent	condominium	uncle	job
friends	itinerary	grandma	travel
outdoors	reservation	grandpa	relax
sleeping bag	travel	mom	vacation
cookout	interstate	dad	visit
duffel bag	restaurant	baby	season
canteen	information	parents	skateboard
knife	destination	adult	park
overnight	arrive	together	picnic
dining hall	depart	relatives	hike
flag	schedule	house	camp
ceremony		apartment	fish
latrine		school	watermelon
		job	outdoors

BASEBALL	FRIEND	SCHOOL	PET
umpire	loyal	friends	habitat
home run	considerate	teachers	food
outfield	kind	classes	train
dugout	humorous	report card	care of
team	creative	books	veterinarian
championship	trustworthy	paper	tame
tournament	athletic	pencils	wild
fly ball	intelligent	education	breed
strike	eager	learn	color
bunt	compassionate	cafeteria	appearance
foul	flexible	recess	shelter
glove	prompt	desk	litter
coach	cheerful	teach	leash
captain	open	principal	master
		secretary	

76

FOOTLONG STORIES

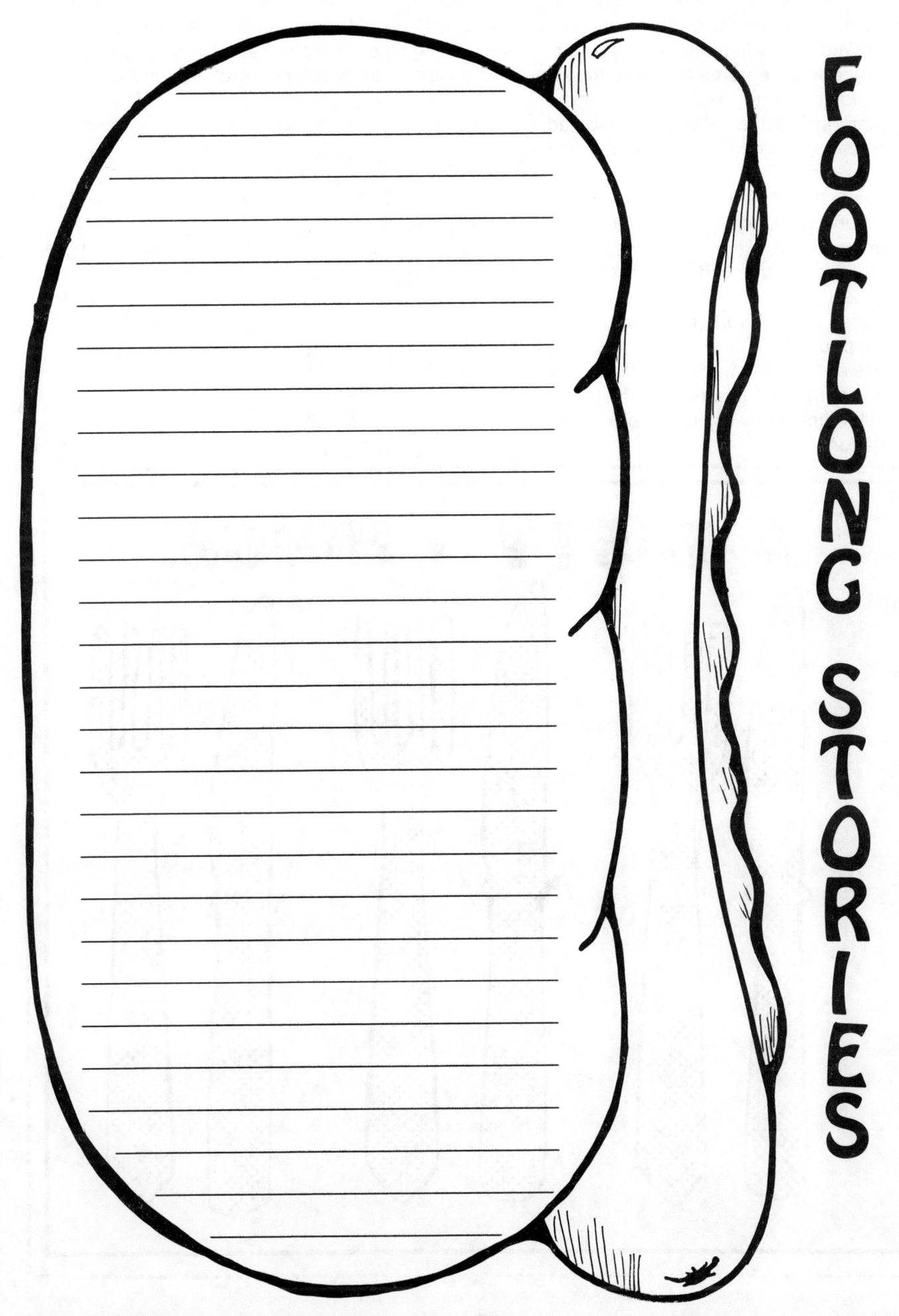

Paste the label below on the cover of a file folder. Use oaktag and duplicate several silverware patterns (page 80). Xerox the character, setting, and plot cards from page 79. Cut apart the cards and glue the character cards to forks, setting cards to knives, and plot cards to spoons. Glue three pockets inside the folder, one labeled *characters*, one labeled *setting*, one labeled *plot*.

Opposite the pockets write these simple directions for students to use to complete the activity:

1. Write your name and the date on your paper.
2. Chose a knife, fork, and spoon from the pockets.
3. Use all three elements to write a story on your paper, complete with title.
4. Place finished work in the box at the station.

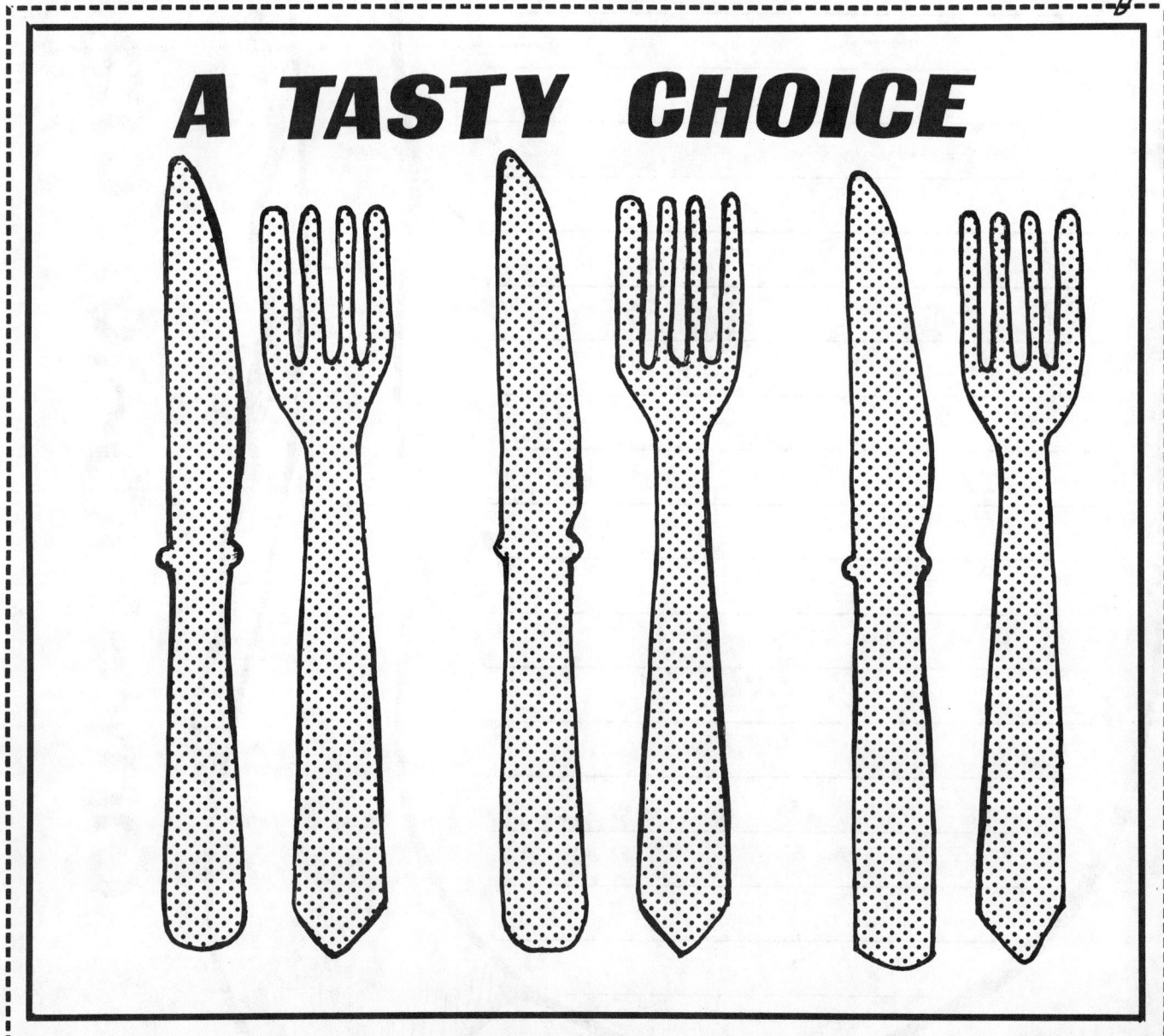

A TASTY CHOICE

Character	Setting	Plot
Dinosaur	at the zoo	having a party
Dog	in the space shuttle	making a movie
Grandma	in a swimming pool	writing a book
Giant	at the beach	setting up a business
Dad	in a skyscraper	exploring at night
Mom	in the woods	searching for clues
Teacher	in a cabin	going on a picnic
Bear	in the jungle	planning a vacation
Rock singer	in a Porsche	building something
Best friend and I	in a haunted house	cooking dinner
Horse	in a cave	inventing something
Alien	in the barn	interviewing for a job
Spider	at school	looking for someone
TV star	in Hollywood	playing a game

A TASTY CHOICE

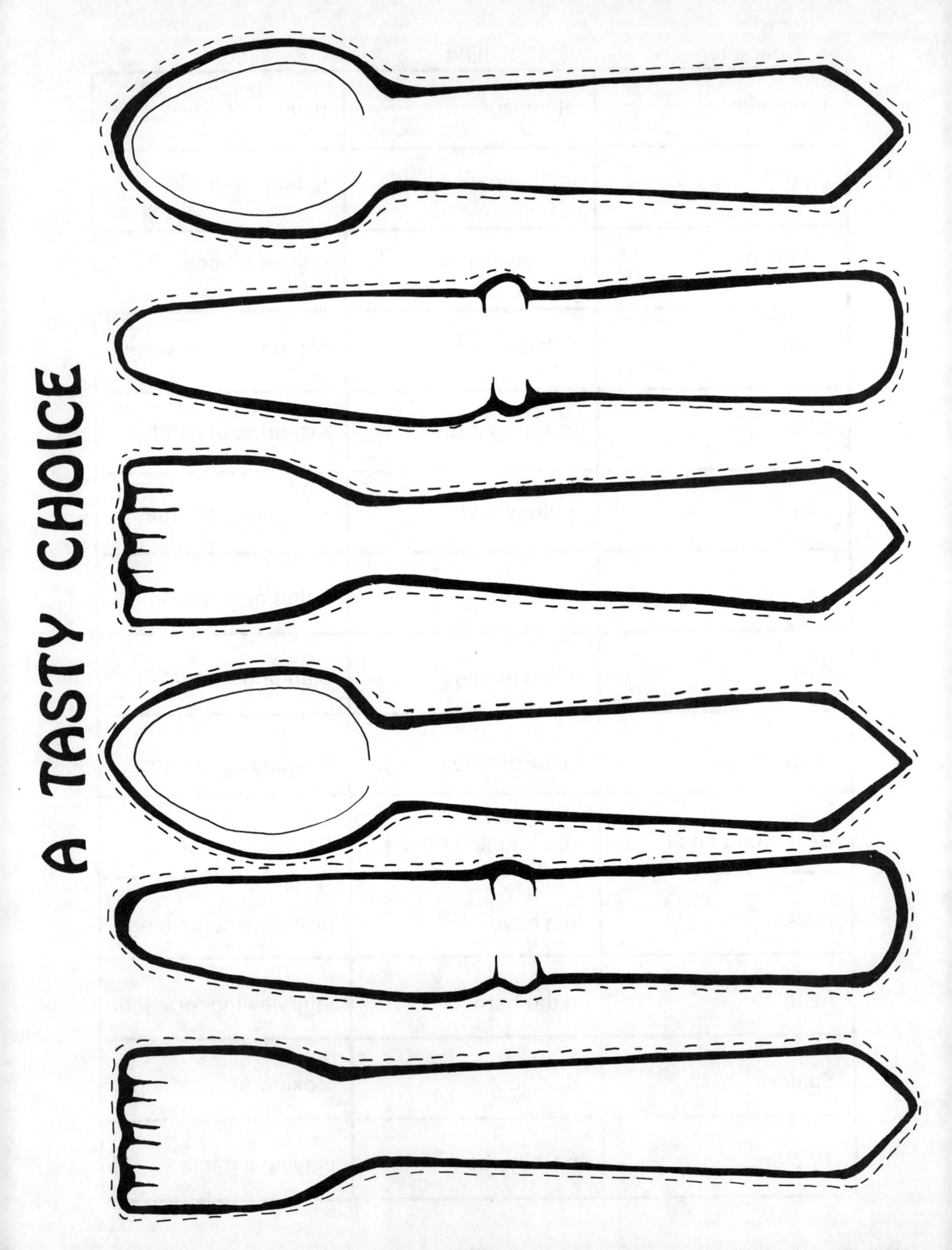

80

ADVENTURE VENTURE

What a catch these delightful mini units will be. They will provide the motivational atmosphere you and your class may be searching for as the school year progresses.

Travellin' Packets can be Xeroxed and sent home to parents to provide a wealth of summer learning experiences in all content areas. Select those activities appropriate to your students. It can be used in the classroom by the teacher to present old materials with a new twist. Simply "plant" the seeds, nurture them, and watch them grow.

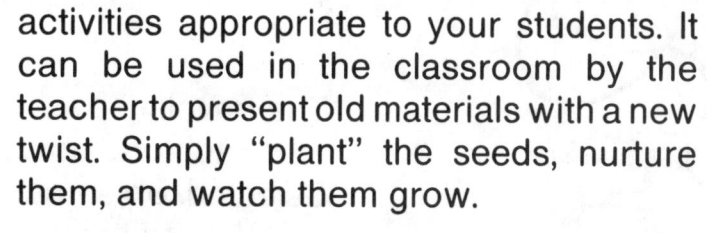

Junior Job Journal creatively combines the themes of the newspaper with the idea of summer jobs. Both teacher and students can explore types of jobs presented here as children complete newspaper activities. Perhaps Junior Job Journal will inspire the students to write their own newspaper.

Duplicate the Summertime Rap and let your class present it to an eager audience. Involve all students in some way as you "rap up" the school year. Use the masks provided, or allow your children to dress as the parts suggest.

TRAVELLIN' PACKETS

The travellin' packets are filled with seeds
    Each one unique and new,
Selected, oh so carefully,
    With things for you to do.
Just take a little seed or two,
    Examine them with care.
Now add a little sunshine here,
    A drop of water there.
And ask a friend to help you
    So it will be lots of fun,
But don't forget to take some time—
    Go out! Enjoy the sun.
And take along the ideas that
    Your teachers gave each day
Spice them up with great advice
    That parents sent your way.
Create a summer garden, plant all
    The seeds you know,
Nourish them with loving thoughts—
    How magically you'll grow!

HOW DOES YOUR GARDEN GROW?

- BOOKS
- NOTES
- SLATES
- MANIPULATIVES
- STUDY BUDDY
- GAMES
- AUDIO VISUALS

LANGUAGE ARTS

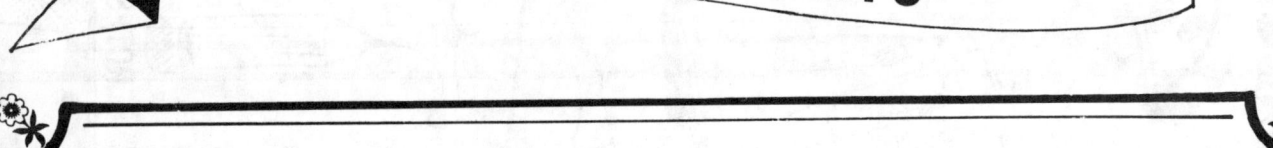

1. Read poetry aloud (Shel Silverstein's *Where the Sidewalk Ends* and the *Light in the Attic* are great; limerick books are humorous; Mother Goose adds rhythm and rhyme children love).
2. Read books aloud at regularly scheduled times (younger children/remedial readers enjoy shorter books or one chapter at a time; older children love ghost stories and are more attentive to more chapters/longer books). Be sure to include classical literature! Reading lists are available from your librarian!
3. Read the newspaper to/with your children.
4. Encourage children to "read" catalogs, "shopping" for items on their wish list.
5. Employ a cook's helper to assist you in reading recipes.
6. Write word labels on objects around the house/classroom to promote correct spelling of everyday words.
7. Give children a map to read on your family vacation. Ask them to find particular places of interest en route.
8. Ask your children to read the labels on grocery store items to find foods with the best nutritional values.
9. Assist children in reading how-to directions for construction of Legos or models.
10. Play word games with your children—Scrabble, Boggle, Hangman.
11. Give children books containing crossword puzzles, word searches, and Mad Lib books (stocking stuffers, birthday favors/gifts).
12. Tell stories to children (great for developing listening/speaking skills).
13. Dictate stories and ask older children to write them, or let younger children dictate, and you record their thoughts.
14. Encourage children to write letters/postcards to friends or relatives.
15. Teach children proper telephone etiquette and encourage them to use it (see next pages).
16. Cut pictures from old magazines to use as story themes. Have children paste one picture on each page in a creative writing booklet. Let them create stories throughout the week. Don't grade these—just read them to see in which language skills the child needs help. In this way you won't discourage the idea of creative expression and the flow of spontaneous thought onto the page.

CALLING CARDS

- Your best friend has called to ask you to spend the night. Discuss your plans.

- Your friend is sick and would like for you to get his homework tomorrow. What will you say?

- Grandpa wants you to go fishing with him tomorrow. Make plans to go with him.

- It's Mom's birthday on Saturday. Call your aunt and invite her and her family.

- You decide to go roller skating with a friend on Friday. Call to invite her.

- Your neighbor wants you to walk his dog. What will you tell him?

- After you've made plans with a friend to go to the mall, your relatives come. Call your friend.

- Explain to the fireman how to get to your house.

1. You are home with the baby-sitter. The caller wants to talk with your parents. What will you say?

2. You are home alone. Your mom will be home from work soon. What will you tell the caller?

3. You are baby-sitting. The parents have just left for the evening. What will you say to the caller?

4. While you are home alone, you receive a prank call. What will you do? What if he calls back?

5. Your mom gets sick. Call a neighbor and explain the problem to her.

6. You answer the phone. Dad is outside working on the car and the call is for him. What should you do?

7. A classmate calls frequently but seems to have nothing to say. What should you tell him?

8. While you are home alone, someone calls and wants you to buy something. What will you say?

9. Someone dialed the wrong number and reached you. What questions should you ask?

WRITING

1. Give your children a diary (they'll love the lock and keys). This will encourage them to record their experiences and feelings.
2. Have children keep a journal of a field trip or family vacation.
3. Place writing topics, story starters, and story endings in a basket. Let children choose something of interest to them.
4. Ask children to copy a poem for you in their best handwriting. Display finished work in a prominent place. Find something good to say about the completed assignment.
5. Let children experiment writing with pen. Often they will try harder because the ink does not erase easily (except Eraser-Mate pens).
6. Allow children to write on the chalkboard. This takes practice too!
7. Encourage children to practice writing numbers. Math requires neatness, especially for certain math skills.
8. Teach children the correct way to address envelopes. Stress form, punctuation, and capitalization.
9. Teach children how to print titles and labels for maps and reports. Centering the title and selecting the proper letter size are two areas to review.
10. Introduce calligraphy to older children. Calligraphy markers are now available and great for beginners. A set of five pens is approximately $5.00 and includes an instructional booklet and carrying case. Another neat stocking stuffer! Many children who are poor writers often become the best calligraphers!
11. For the next birthday party, ask your children to do the cake decorating! First experiment with writing with icing or shaving cream on waxed paper. Cupcakes or flat cookies also allow for fun experimenting!
12. Try some ghost writing. Place some lemon juice in a small container. Give children Q-tips and let them write messages with them on paper. Place them in the sun so the writing can develop. Some office supply stores now carry actual ghost writing markers with developers.
13. Work with children on a regular basis to develop proper handwriting techniques. Most schools have a writing workbook for children to use. Select ideas from these to stress at home.
14. Give children puppets and encourage them to create a script (see following pages).

Butterfly Puppet

Have a little fun! Cut out the butterfly and sunflower puppets. Color them before you glue them to paper sacks.

With a friend, write a script for the puppet play. Present it to an anxious audience. Add other puppets of your own if you like.

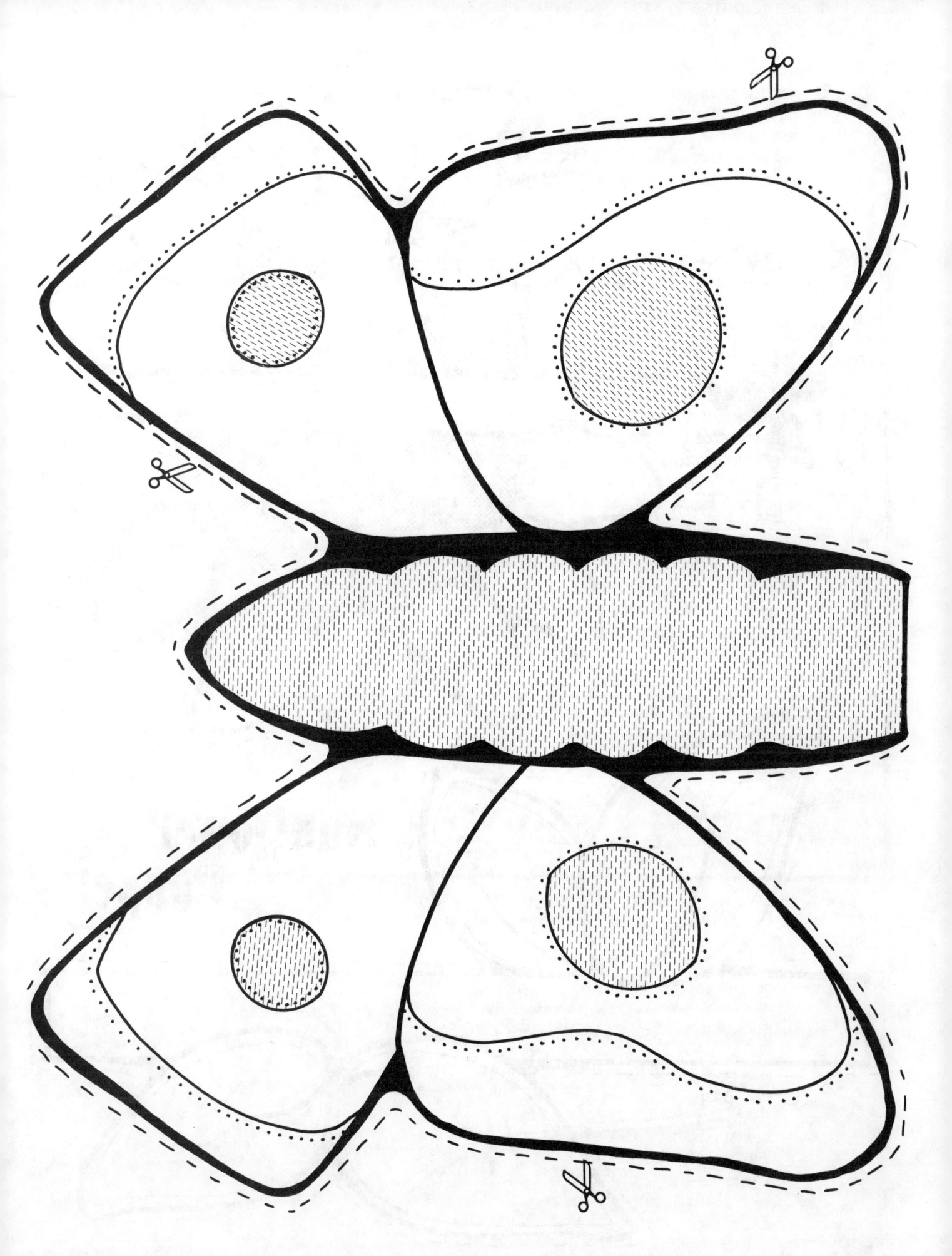

89

Sunflower Puppet

90

GA1145

Copyright © 1990, Good Apple, Inc.

SCIENCE

1. Visit a farm to observe crops and/or animals. Discuss questions your children have with the farmer or farmhands.
2. Plant a garden of your own. Be sure to water, weed, and harvest it!
3. Get a pet. Read about it first so that you will know how to care for it properly. A trip to the vet is a great learning experience.
4. Make a weather calendar with your children. Record weather, temperature, etc., on it. You may find weather stickers for the calendar at a local card shop (see page 93).
5. Visit a zoo. Make a list with the children of the kinds of animals there. Describe their habitats. Talk to the zookeepers.
6. Take children on a walk through an aviary or conservatory. Be sure to ask a friend along!
7. Stop at the local pet store. This is a nice way to enjoy animals if your children cannot have pets.
8. Go on a fossil dig. Place several Baggies and a magnifying glass in a small backpack. A canteen of water, snack, and camera might be nice, too!
9. Ask children to don old sneakers and take them on a creek hike. Choose a creek familiar to you.
10. Take your children on a moonlight walk to gaze at the stars. Can you identify different constellations?
11. Go for a walk through an arboretum or the woods. See how many trees you can recognize by their bark, by their leaves, and by their fruit. Fall is a spectacular time for this!
12. Get a microscope. Let children examine different objects under the lens (sand, salt, sugar, newsprint, and hair are a few good choices).
13. Start a collection. Suggestions include insects and rocks.
14. Ask children to make bicycle/skateboard safety posters to color and display.
15. Make several kinds of paper airplanes. Let your children experiment with them to see which ones fly best. Have a paper airplane contest!
16. Build rockets or parachutes with your children. Have a Space Day!

PUMPKIN PATCH FUN

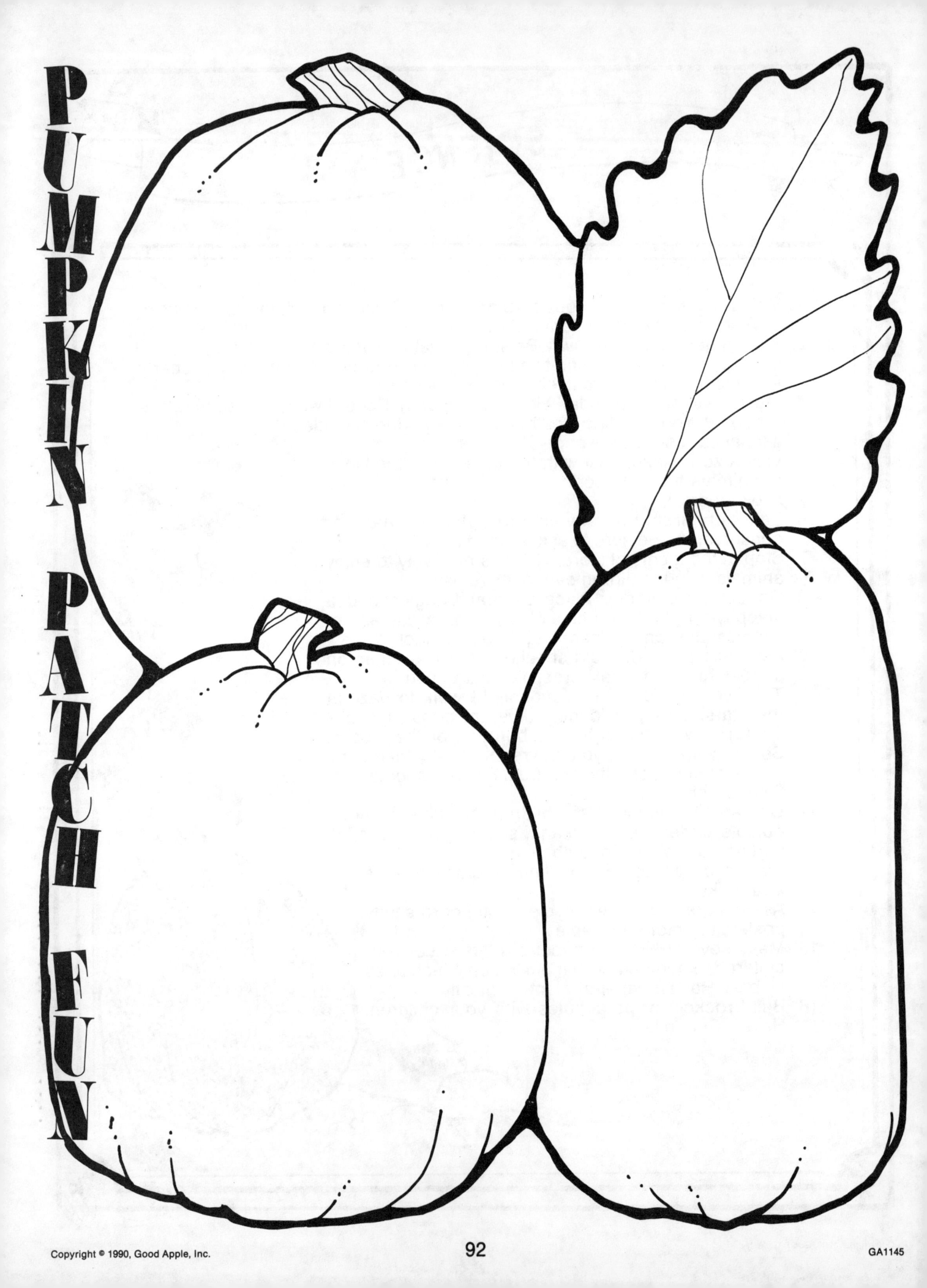

SAT.				
FRI.				
THURS.				
WED.				
TUES.				
MON.				
SUN.				

TELEVISION

1. As a family, sit down together and contract time for use of the TV. Before completing the schedule, stress to everyone the importance of being selective in choosing a program, and that once decisions are made, they are to be kept. Curtail use of the TV so that viewing is premium entertainment (see next page).
2. Ask your children to write down three good commercials and be able to explain why they are superior.
3. After viewing a program, ask your children to state the main idea in sentence form.
4. Have children select a character from their favorite TV show and write a paragraph explaining why they admire that person.
5. Expose your children to various types of television shows (entertainment, humor, suspense, drama, news, etc.).
6. Encourage your family to watch the news together. Discuss events with children. Keep them familiar with people and places in current events.
7. Have your children watch educational TV. There are numerous programs for most curricular areas. Some TV game shows are also educational!
8. Teach your children how to use the *TV Guide.*

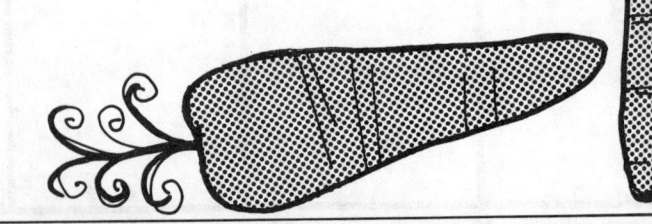

TIME	SUN	MON	TUES	WED	THURS	FRI	SAT
9 - 10 AM							
10 - 11							
11 - 12							
12 - 1 PM							
1 - 2							
2 - 3							
3 - 4							
4 - 5							
5 - 6							
6 - 7							
7 - 8							
8 - 9							
9 - 10							

MATH

1. Assist your children with completing order forms from their favorite catalogs.
2. Produce a family of cooks. Call for helping hands to double, triple, or reduce recipes. The whole gang will feel pleased.
3. Teach your children how to compute distance/gas mileage on trips.
4. Play games which use money. This makes children more comfortable counting and spending money.
5. Go on a shape hunt. Select a particular shape and see who can find the most objects with that shape. Or divide the group and let each group find objects with a certain shape (this can also be done using magazines indoors).
6. Create pictures using particular shapes.
7. Children love playing cards. Shuffling and dealing cards requires coordination. Playing cards reinforces the skills of counting, keeping score, sequence, greater than/less than, taking turns, and sportsmanship.
8. With your authorization, let children practice dialing the phone numbers of relatives and friends.
9. Introduce liquid measurement in your swimming pool or the kitchen sink. Have children experiment with gallons, quarts, pints, and cups; try metric measures, too!
10. Play the game of Battleship with children. This game reinforces the concept of coordinates (see next page).
11. Make graphs with your children of favorite foods, books read during the week/month, and money earned during the summer.
12. Ask your family to create a TV schedule that includes requests of all family members.
13. When traveling through different time zones, introduce this concept to your children.

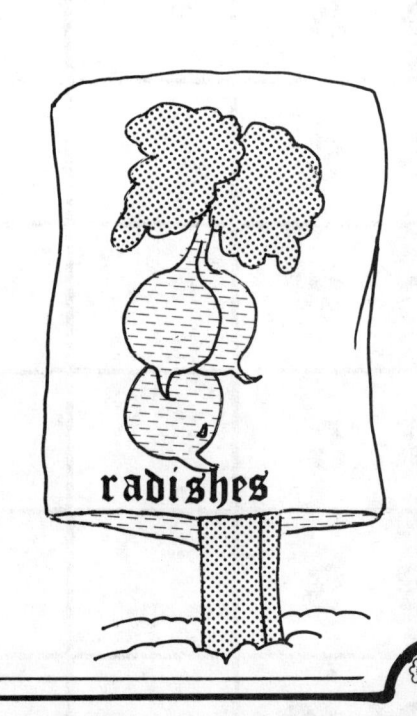

DOT TO DOT

Create a game! Battleship! Magic Picture! Coordinates! Cross-Stitch a Design! Geoboard! Name Squares!

MEASURE FOR PLEASURE

Teaching measurement can be fun. Begin with an object such as your hand. Show children that they can use their hands to decide how long or how tall something is. Measure a table with your hand. Let children measure a few objects with you using your hands. Once children learn the concept of measurement, let them experiment independently or with a buddy.

Try measuring with these:
1. Feet
2. Carrot
3. Pencil
4. String (cut to a specific length)
5. Finger
6. Book
7. Strip of paper
8. Ruler
9. Yardstick
10. Meterstick
11. Cup/Bowl
12. Spoon

Set up a corner in your room where children can experiment with wet/dry, solid/liquid, and standard/metric measurement.

The sandbox or the swimming pool are great places to begin! Encourage children to record their heights using different measures. Create small lists of objects for children to measure using particular objects. Send them on a Measure Hunt which you have designed. They will love it!

Have your children record their height and weight at regular intervals. Ask them to record the date in a small notebook for future reference. Teach them how to graph this information.

PHYS. ED.

1. Attend a local/pro game with your family. Discuss skills necessary to make good athletes. Watch for these during the event.
2. Teach a sport you know to someone. Be sure to explain the rules!
3. Study a famous athlete. Collect information about him/her and present it on a poster. Place it where others will see it.
4. Collect baseball or football cards. Trade them with friends.
5. Join a league—T-ball, baseball, bowling, football, basketball. Keep your body in shape and stay healthy! Practice!
6. Exercise regularly. Use a calendar or chart to record your exercise schedule. Also monitor your weight.
7. Learn to play a new sport. Many colleges have athletes from other countries who would be willing to teach others a sport from their hometown.
8. Practice skills regularly: hop, skip, jump, slide, bounce, dribble, turn, twist. Always remember to stretch carefully before beginning any workout.
9. Practice throwing and catching balls of various sizes, shapes, and weights (beanbags, footballs, softballs, baseballs, Nerf balls, racquetballs, etc.).
10. Play games with others. Remember to practice all of the cooperation skills of good sportsmanship, taking turns, sharing, and selecting games others want to play.
11. Remember to exercise your pet, too! Take your pet or a neighbor's for a walk. Give him water!
12. Plan an activity day based on a theme and invite the neighborhood (see next page).

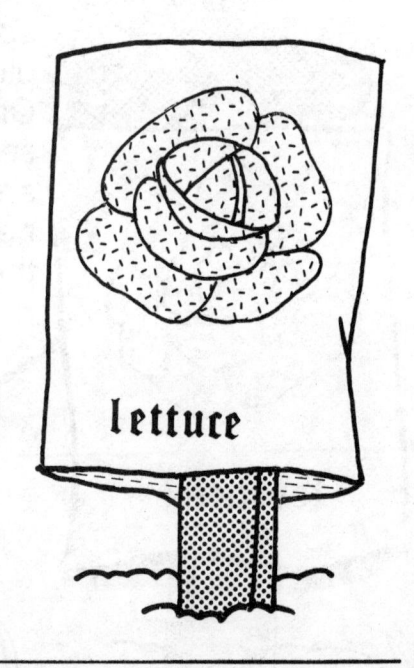

LET US PARTY!

Plan a Backyard Carnival. Set up food, games, music, rides. Decorate with balloons. Add a clown for atmosphere. Invite the neighborhood.

Get in the act. Plan a Drama Day to keep the excitement going. Practice choral readings, puppet plays, dances, songs, and skits. Involve even the youngest. Ticket takers are in good demand.

A Splash Bash is sure to draw a crowd on a hot summer day. Ask guests to bring beach towels, radios, sunglasses and lotion. Furnish the pool (or water slide) and squirt bottles.

Don't forget the Sock Hop. Get tapes or play records from the 50's. Provide a slick floor and refreshments.

An Olympic Day of sport events will please all of the kids. Organize games and select the judges. Food and ribbons for winners will be a hit with the gang.

Organize a Magic Show. Get a book with tricks of all kinds. Add the props. Let the magic begin.

lettuce

ART

1. Take your children to an art museum. Be sure to stop in the gift shop and purchase postcards or a coloring book of the museum's art. Mail completed pictures to friends.
2. Learn to draw, watercolor, or paint. It's something the whole family can enjoy. Have an art show at the family reunion.
3. Play Pictionary with your children.
4. Learn to sew or do stitchery (embroidery, needlepoint, crewel).
5. Design a doll outfit, either from paper or cloth.
6. Learn a new craft, or teach others a craft you know. Set up a craft show for others to see.
7. Pick fresh flowers and arrange them in a vase for your dining room table.
8. Assign children a particular artist to research. Ask them to share their findings with others.
9. Design a card. Write your own verse and mail it to someone special (see next page).
10. Make several small favors with a friend. Deliver them to a hospital or nursing home.
11. Create your own stationery. Stencil a matching envelope.
12. Decorate your bedroom. Catalog pictures will help you coordinate curtains, bedding, carpet, walls, accessories, and furniture.

CREATE A CARD

Materials:
1. Tulip card and pattern made from construction paper
2. Crayons or markers
3. Glue
4. Scissors
5. Pencil or pen

Directions:
1. Cut out and color the tulip card and pattern.
2. Fold the tulip as illustrated, bending the petals outward.
3. Write a verse on the inside of the tulip. Be sure to sign your name.
4. Glue the tulip onto the card.
5. Give the card to someone special.

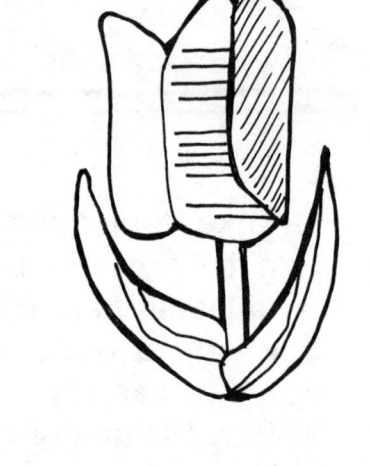

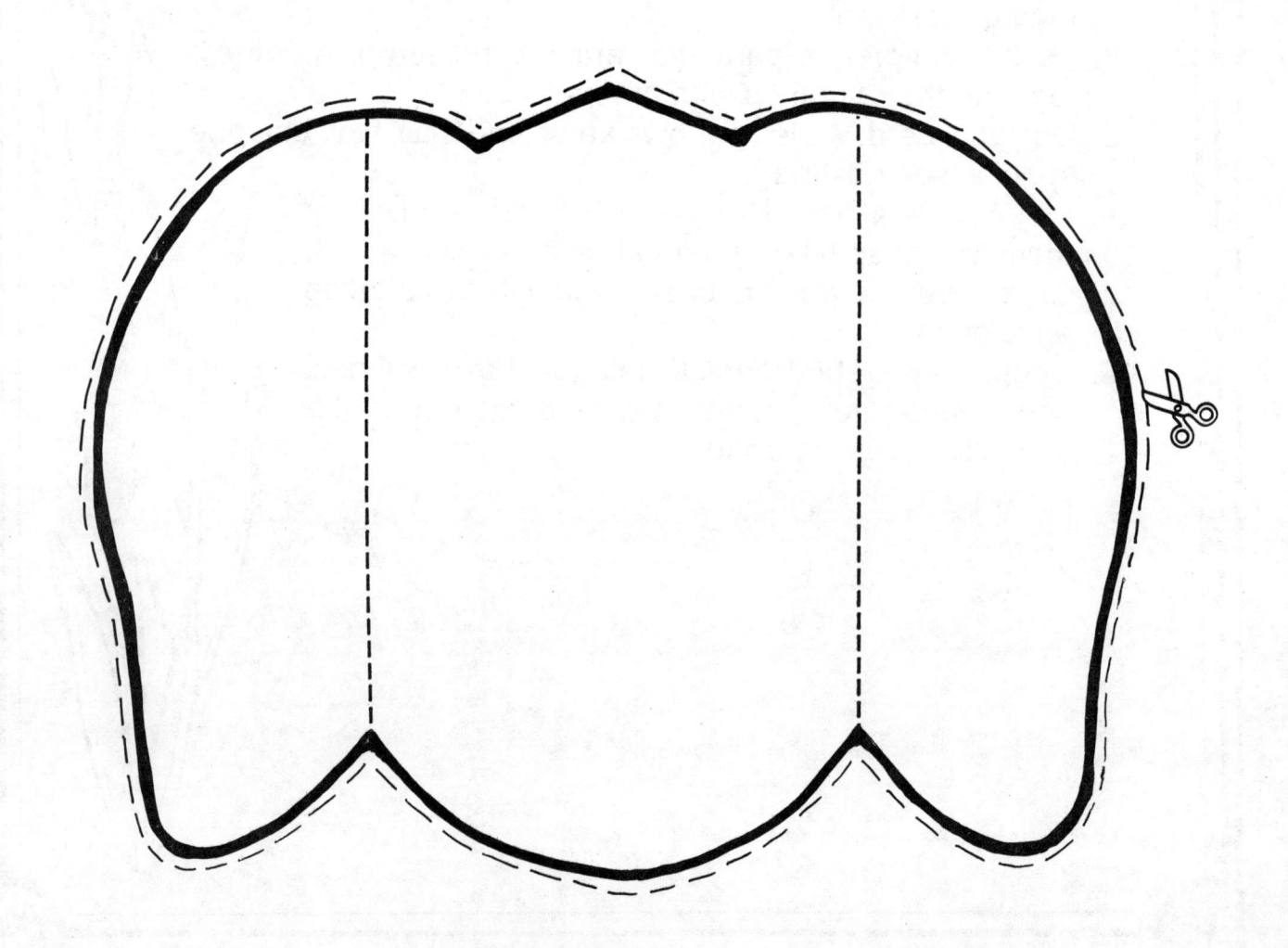

GLUE HERE

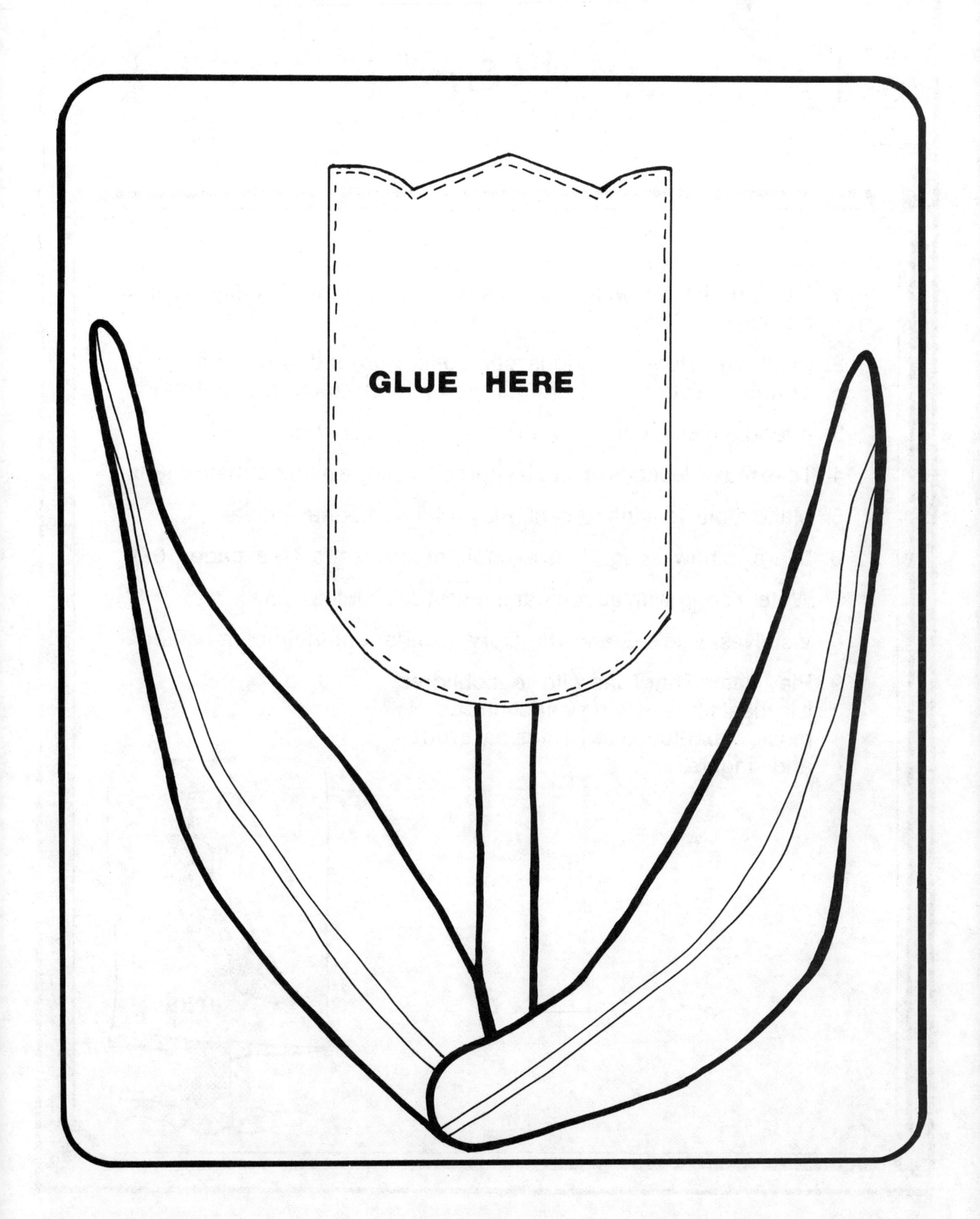

MUSIC

1. Fill your house with all types of music. Play it softly during mealtime.

2. Display posters of various composers around your classroom or house. Label each. Encourage children to learn about them.

3. Attend a music concert with your family or friends.

4. Take music lessons or teach yourself to play a musical instrument.

5. Make a musical instrument. Play it for someone special.

6. Learn a new song. Join a choir or orchestra (see page 107).

7. Write a song with accompaniment. Teach it to others.

8. Visit Nashville's Grand Ole Opry or other entertainment centers.

9. Play Name That Tune with your children. It is ideal for reviewing Christmas carols, music of particular eras, musical groups, and singers.

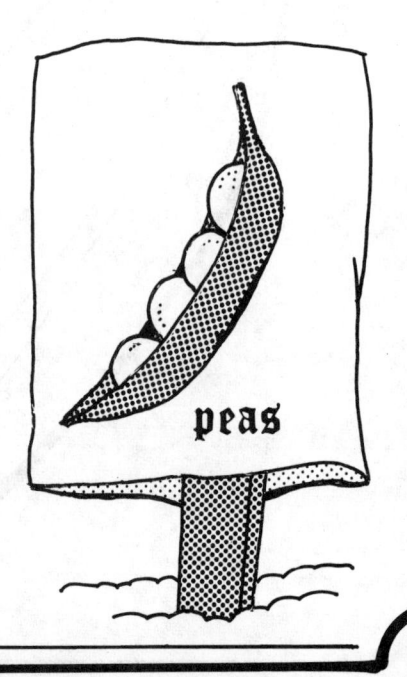

PRESENTING

LIGHTS! CAMERA! ACTION!

Use oaktag or heavy paper to create this seed packet stage and the stick puppets (see page 106). Cut along the dotted lines. Color the puppets if you like. Insert the puppets into the pea shell. Practice moving the peas in the shell.

Practice singing the song "Four Little Peas" (page 107) with a friend. Present your skit to others.

CUT ALONG DOTTED LINE

SINGING PUPPETS

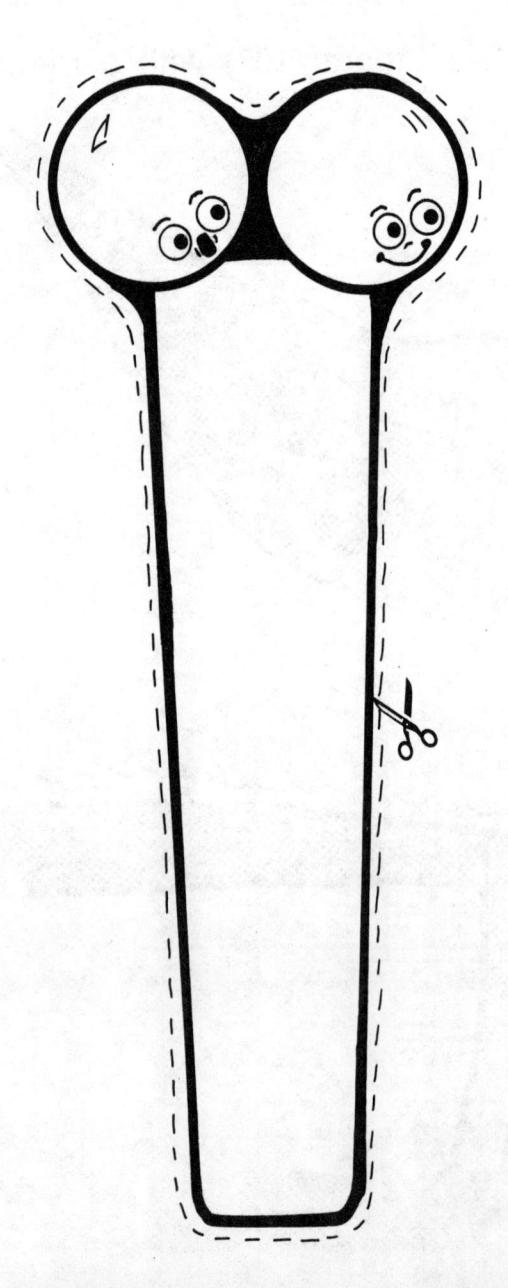

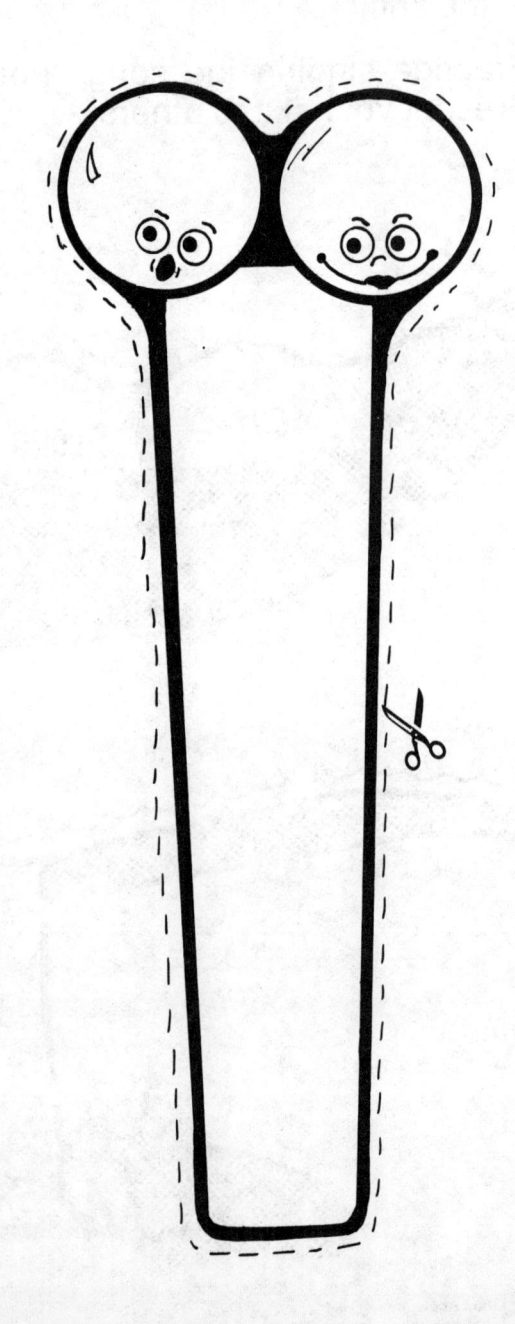

Four Little Peas
(Sing to tune of "Six Little Ducks")

Four little peas that I once knew,
Round ones, plump ones, skinny ones too.
'Cause the two little peas sittin' cozy in the shell
Surely can sing and dance so well.

Early in the morn when the sun does rise
They do yawn and roll their eyes
'Cause the two little peas sittin' cozy in the shell
Surely can sing and dance so well.

They stretch their arms and reach so high
Wave a wave to the butterfly
'Cause the two little peas sittin' cozy in the shell
Surely can sing and dance so well.

Their legs do wiggle, their feet go tap
Listen softly, hear them rap
'Cause the two little peas sittin' cozy in the shell
Surely can sing and dance so well.

They've got the beat, they're movin' fast
Boogie down, boogie down, havin' a blast.
'Cause the two little peas sittin' cozy in the shell
Surely can sing and dance so well.

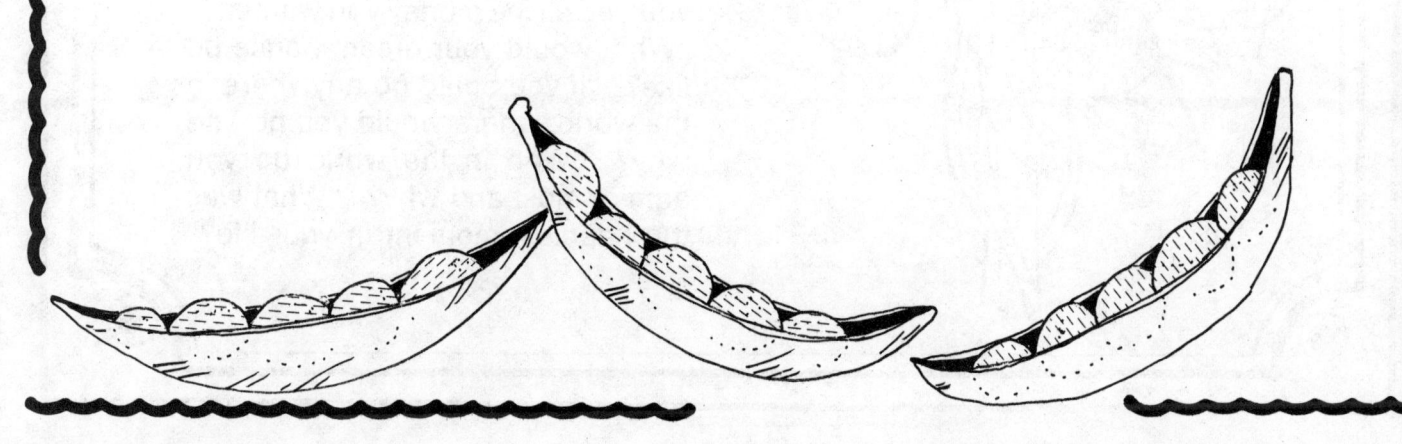

SHARE TIME

1. Sit down with your family and share picture albums, home movies, slides, and tapes. Reminisce about family vacations, family gatherings, and relatives.

2. Plan a vacation together. Keep in mind the length of time you have to spend, finances, ages of those going, and interests of the individual family members.

3. Share information about the family background. Begin a family tree.

4. Attend your family reunion. If your family does not have a reunion, start the tradition yourself. Be selective about where it is held.

5. Visit a park. Enjoy the outdoors.

6. Go on a picnic. Let the children plan the food and activities.

7. Play a game with your children. Design a gameboard complete with game cards and rules. Add a title (see page 110).

8. Tell jokes; make up riddles. Write these down in a little book of your own. Staple in extra pages for later ideas (see page 109).

9. Build a tree house or make a playhouse. Furnish it!

10. Make a tent indoors. Read a book inside, have lunch, take a nap, play. Enjoy the privacy!

11. Work a jigsaw puzzle. Start it on a table or other area where it can be left undisturbed.

12. As a family, talk about your dreams and goals.

13. Fantasize—"What would you do if you had all the money you wanted?" "What would your dream house be like?" "If you could go anywhere in the world, where would you go and why?" "Who in the world do you admire most and why?" "What was the happiest moment in your life?"

"TOE"riffic Riddles

1. What kind of jelly do toes like on toast?
    Toe Jam

2. What kind of Mexican food do toes like most?
    Burritos

3. What snack food do toes like best?
    Fritos

4. What is the favorite plant of toes?
    Mistletoe

5. What two foods do toes like to eat?
    Potatoes, Tomatoes

6. On what kind of sleds do toes like to ride?
    "To"boggans

7. Why did the toe go into the hardware store?
    To buy some "toe"nails

8. How did the toe pay for his bus ride?
    With a Token

9. Where do toes live?
    Toledo, Topeka, Toronto

10. What city in Japan do toes visit most?
    Tokyo

11. What kind of job do most toes have?
    Topographer

12. What was Romeo's famous line in *Romeo and Juliet*?
    Toe be or not toe be; that is the question

13. How did the toe die?
    Ptomaine Poisoning

14. What planet do toes like best?
    Pluto

15. Where do toes keep their pictures?
    Photo Albums

Now it's your turn. Choose a word and create riddles of your own.

START

END

110

GA1145

USE
JUNIOR JOB JOURNAL

* To identify various elements of a newspaper (Types of stories, ads, photos, letters, comics)

* To develop an awareness of various types of employment for children through reading and discussing the articles (Library helper, lawn caretaker, pet sitter, writer, baby-sitter, party entertainer, concession stand clerk, recycler, newspaper carrier, inventor, photographer. Include other jobs children mention to add to those in the newspaper.)

* To encourage self-realization about qualities, skills, and responsibilities students bring to their jobs

* To encourage children to read the newspaper for humor as well as information
(Skim/Scan)

* To discuss risks that are part of all jobs

* To review particular aspects of language
(Proper/common nouns; types of sentences; synonyms, antonyms, homonyms; main idea; topic sentence; word attack—suffixes, prefixes, root words, syllabication, context clues; punctuation; parts of speech)

* To summarize articles and interpret them for others
(Comprehension)

JUNIOR JOB JOURNAL

Saturday, April 3, 1989   Youth, West Virginia   15¢

Boy Becomes Millionaire

By Craig Hoff
Job Journal Staff Writer
Invent, America—Early Friday morning reporters gathered at the home of Rusty Clippers. For a school project, Rusty designed a "super" lawn mower, which he calls "Lawn Man." This incredible machine not only mows grass, but it also collects leaves and other small debris. Lawn Man's stunning attachments also enable it to trim shrubs and hedges, edge sidewalks, and clip around close objects. Judges from the Invent, America contest will be at Mt. Harmony School on May 1 to present Rusty and his teacher their awards. Rusty states that he is looking forward to using his Lawn Man this summer. He will be at Grassy Run Mall on May 6 to demonstrate his latest invention.

CLOSE CALL

By Adam Conan
Chow City—A nine-year-old girl escaped serious injuries last evening as she played outside her home. A chow, owned by Harry Paugh, escaped from his dogsitter and bit the young girl several times on the leg. She was admitted to P.E.T. Hospital where she was treated and later released. No charges have been filed against the owner or the dogsitter.

Garden Club Membership Growing

By Trisha Torrie
Garden Press
Bloomer—Daisy Hill Garden Club met at the home of Rhoda Dendron on Saturday, March 27. New members enrolled were Rosie Bush and Chris San Themum. Mrs. Dendron's lecture about planting and fertilizing was very informative. Guest speaker Bud Ing treated the members to a floral show, displaying a variety of his own prize plants. The next meeting is scheduled for May 15. Members and their friends are welcome to attend the meeting. The date, time, and place will be announced.

New Business Opens

By Michael Mann

Moose, Oregon—Have you heard the latest? Two brothers have teamed up to form a new business called "Humor Us." If you are planning a birthday party, backyard barbecue, or just an ordinary party, be sure to request these fellows to entertain your guests. They provide singing, dancing, comedy acts, and lots more when they appear at your party in costume. Please suggest to them your party theme, and they will turn your social gathering into a most memorable experience. For more information, just call 1-LET-USP-ARTY.

Winners Selected

Pet Patrol Winners: (left to right) Ellie Funt, Sally Mander, Bob White, Kattie Did, Paul Parrot, and Jim Panzee. Photo by Germaine Shepherd.

Patrol Trip Planned

Busses will arrive at Zooberg Elementary at 8:30 a.m. to transport the winners of the Pet Patrol to Washington, D.C., for their annual trip to the capital. The trip itinerary includes a visit to the Washington Zoo, tour of U.S.A. Veterinary Hospital, a stop at the Dog House, and finally a private tour of the Purina factory. Parents may pick up their children at the school at 5:30 p.m.

Help for Working Moms

By Kimberly Ann
Send your children to the newest child care center in town. Directed by Kitty Sitter, the program provides summer fun for children ages 3-12. Indoor and outdoor activities, field trips, and a variety of lessons will be on the agenda to make this the best summer for your child. Enrollment is limited, so act now!

Junior Job Journal

Junior Job Journal is looking for enthusiastic youths who like a challenge. The contest is open to newspaper carriers ages 10-18 who are eager to earn money, dependable, and cheerful. Applicants must have sturdy legs, strong arms, and a sense of humor. Please call Junior Job Journal for more information. Phone 296-READ.

Dear Adella

Dear Adella,
The children in our neighborhood have nowhere to ride bicycles or skateboards. We have a park nearby with paths, but there is no paved area. What can we do?

Jeremy

Dear Jeremy,
Perhaps if all of your friends and their parents got together, you could develop a plan for fund-raising. Suggest the ideas to the Parks and Recreation committee and see if they can help you.

Dear Adella,
I am twelve years old and bored. My brothers play Little League ball and I have to go to the park and watch them play. Any ideas?

Tina

Dear Tina,
Try to get a job at the concession stand.

GRAND OPENING MAY 12
KIDDIEROBICS

LOOKING FOR A JOB?
Take My Advice

By Aaron Nicola

West Side—Now is the time to be thinking seriously about a job, whether it is for summer employment or for an extended period. First, decide what type of job you would like: indoor/outdoor; physical/mental; office/waiting on customers; large/small business; full/part-time. Next, decide how you will get to work. Will you walk, drive, bike, find transportation with a parent or neighbor, or ride the bus? Third, find out what qualifications are required. Do you fit the job description? Fourth, inquire about the pay. Is it hourly, weekly, by the month, or tips? Finally, decide if this is the way you would happily spend your time earning money. Can you find ways to make and keep the job enjoyable?

Once you have considered answers to the questions above, select the job in which you feel you can give your best effort. Go for it!

I Got the Job! Now What?

The first day of work is here and I'm scared to death. I've waited a long time to find the perfect job, and now . . . If these are your fears, you're not alone. Many people start their first day of work feeling as you do. Here are some tips.

1. Get a good night's sleep.
2. Allow yourself plenty of time to dress properly and arrive safely.
3. Listen closely to the instructions your boss gives you.
4. Take your job seriously, and accept the responsibilities that go with it.
5. Be mannerly and cheerful at all times.
6. Enjoy the experience.
7. Save your earnings. Spend wisely.

SAVE, SAVE

By Melissa Cole
Rainbow Press

Alumtown—Don't miss the chance! Earn extra money the easy way. Just save those empty aluminum cans, glass bottles, and old newspapers. Store them in heavy-duty garbage bags. Bring your collection to your local supermarket where Rhea Cycle will pay you. Thanks for helping to keep Alumtown clean.

WEATHER

SUNNY 75°

PET PEEVES

By Deborah Michelle

Knoxville—In a recent survey, we have discovered that property owners are quite disturbed by pesky little critters some folks call pets. Here are the most commonly reported pet peeves.
1. Masters allow their pets to roam neighborhoods freely without supervision.
2. Owners do not dress their pets appropriately for the weather.
3. Pets litter and do not clean up their messes (nor do their owners).
4. Animals pollute the area with unnecessary noise.
5. Masters allow pets to dig for their dinner in freshly planted gardens.
6. Owners are not registering their pets at the courthouse.
7. Masters are not getting their pets examined regularly by a veterinarian. Most pets require shots when they are young.

Library Announces New Program

By Heather Rex
Job Journal Staff Writer

Fairmont—Shannon Public Library will feature a new program for preschoolers. Each Tuesday, beginning May 3, from 10:00 a.m. to 11:00 a.m. parents may bring their children to the library for story hour. Rita Book has prepared several delightful sessions which include stories, movies, puppet plays, games, and make-and-take projects. Please register your child at the main desk at the library by May 10. There is no charge for the program.

Letters to the Editor

Dear Editor,
Thanks to this community for giving its youth a chance to work. Friends and neighbors have provided us with lots of jobs. What an experience we have had this summer.
     Sarah J.

Dear Editor,
I feel there should be more playground equipment at the park. We always have our family reunion there, and there isn't much to do.
     A.N.

Dear Editor,
The traveling soccer team is planning a trip to the state tournament. We need the help of businesses in the community.
     R. Collins

WRITERS WANTED

By Wanda Leonard

Arbors—The local nursing home is looking for talented writers who have some time to share. Many residents need assistance with reading their mail and/or answering it. If you have a little extra time and a lot of patience, please consider helping us with this worthy cause.

Ann's Photos

79 Blueprint Blvd.
507-0689   (phone)

WANT ADS.........

FOR SALE:
16" Huffy bike in good condition. Call 363-4507.

One pair girl's white roller skates. Like new. Call 278-0907.

One-man backpack tent. Used once. Call 367-1200.

Three calico kittens. Six weeks old. $5.00 for all three. Call 363-6564.

WANTED:
Yard work in the east side area. I have my own tools. Call 367-4112.

Baby-sitting in my home or yours. I have references. Please call 366-9875.

Ken and Barbie dolls and accessories in good condition. Call 278-7463.

Why aren't elephants well-paid?

Answer: Because they work for peanuts.

A Scavenger Hunt

_____   _____
(name)   (date)

1. From what city does this newspaper come? _____
2. How much does this newspaper cost? _____
3. Name the animals for sale in the want ads. _____
   How much do they cost? _____
4. Who wrote the article about the library? _____
   _____
5. On what date was the newspaper printed? _____
6. Name the students going to Washington, D.C. _____
   _____
7. Name the owner of the dog that bit the little girl. _____
   _____
8. Name two pet peeves listed in the survey given. _____
   _____
9. What are four things that children can do during story hour? _____
   _____
10. Which two jobs are suggested in the want ads? _____
    _____
11. What type of job is the nursing home requesting? _____
    _____
12. Name three people who were at the Garden Club meeting. _____
    _____
13. Who is director of the new child care program? _____
    _____
14. What size bicycle is for sale? _____
15. What number would you call for entertainment at your party? _____
    _____
16. Who invented the Lawn Man? _____
17. From which city does Deborah Michelle report? _____
18. For which agency does Trisha Torrie write? _____

JOB APPLICATION
(Please print.)

Name _____

Address _____

_____

_____

Phone _____ Birthday _____

Social Security # _____

EDUCATION

School _____ Dates _____

_____ _____

_____ _____

_____ _____

_____ _____

Clubs _____

_____

Offices held _____

_____

Awards _____

_____

WORK EXPERIENCE

Place _____ Dates _____

_____ _____

_____ _____

References (not relatives)

_____

_____

_____

_____ _____
(parent signature)   (parent address)

_____ _____
(your signature)   (today's date)

Summertime Rap

All:
(no masks)   In the summertime
when school is out
We can play outside
and run and shout.
When the sun comes up,
there's lots to do—
We'd like to share our
thoughts with you.

Swimmers: Deep in the water we swim around,
In a pool or in a lake where fish abound.
We dive and kick and snorkel and float—
Perhaps water ski behind a motorboat.
Splish, splash; Splish, splash.

Beach Bums: (whistle) Wh-wh we whistle when the boys go by
As we lie on our towels underneath a blue sky,
With the radio on we listen to the beat,
Catching rays as the sand sifts through our feet.
Wh-wh (whistle); Wh-wh (whistle)

Computer Whizzes: Plug it in, turn it on, push the disc in tight.
Boot it up, watch the screen, then do everything right.
IBM, Texas Instrument, or Apple IIe,
Just give me a computer, I'm a whiz, you'll see!
Beep, beep; Beep, beep.

Athletes: We are hikers, we are bikers, on a motorcycle ride.
We are just the kind of kids who love to be outside.
We fish, hunt, swim, play tennis on a court.
You just name it—we like every kind of sport.
Three strikes; You're out!

Couch Potatoes: We stumble out of bed and then amble to the sofa
Where we lie all day—do nothing but loaf-a
Maybe hit remote control, turn on the TV.
We are perfect couch potatoes, just watch and see!
Crunch, crunch; Slurp, slurp.

Workers: We're the money-making bunch, we get up at dawn,
Go to baby-sit kids, or to mow a new lawn,
Deliver papers to the neighbors, get the Joneses' mail,
Set up a lemonade stand, or have a yard sale.
Big bucks. Yea! Yea!

Travelers: To the relatives house in O-hio
In the car my entire family goes,
Or to Epcot Center, 'cross the Golden Gate Bridge.
Sometimes stay at home and make a trip to the fridge.
We're broke—No joke!

All:
(use masks from each group)
You can see that no matter what the summertime brings,
Our lives are full of these wonderful things.
No hustle, no bustle, no schedule to meet.
You can see that being kids just can't be beat!
Un-uh. No way!

Copyright © 1990, Good Apple, Inc.

Props:
1. A mask for each child.
2. Costumes appropriate to each group.
3. Simple objects suitable for each group.

Notes:
1. You may wish to add a simple motion or noise for certain groups to do, especially when they recite the last line of their part.
2. Use additional masks if you have students who wish to create supplemental lines/parts.
3. Delete lines/masks if you have students who do not choose the parts provided.
4. Have individual groups practice their lines several times so that the rap moves fluently.
5. Ask children to pause between the two sections of their last line in the rap.
6. Give every child a boy or girl mask. All children except travellers will need additional masks for their parts. The swim mask and glasses will be glued onto the face. The computer screen and couch potato designs are to be glued on as hats. The athlete's hat will be folded like a visor before gluing on the band. The bow tie of the worker will be pinned onto the student's shirt at the collar.

Comments:

BOY

Make each boy in the class a copy of the mask using sturdy paper. Have him decorate it to his liking. This will be the only mask worn by students who wish to be travellers. Other students will wear a partial mask over the boy mask.

Copyright © 1990, Good Apple, Inc.

GA1145

GIRL

Make a copy of the mask for each girl in the class using sturdy paper. Have her decorate it to her liking. This will be the only mask worn by students who wish to be travellers. Other students will wear a partial mask over the girl mask.

Copyright © 1990, Good Apple, Inc.

124

GA1145

Swimmer

Beach Bum

Copyright © 1990, Good Apple, Inc. 125 GA1145

fold on dotted line

GLUE to MASK

Athlete

Worker

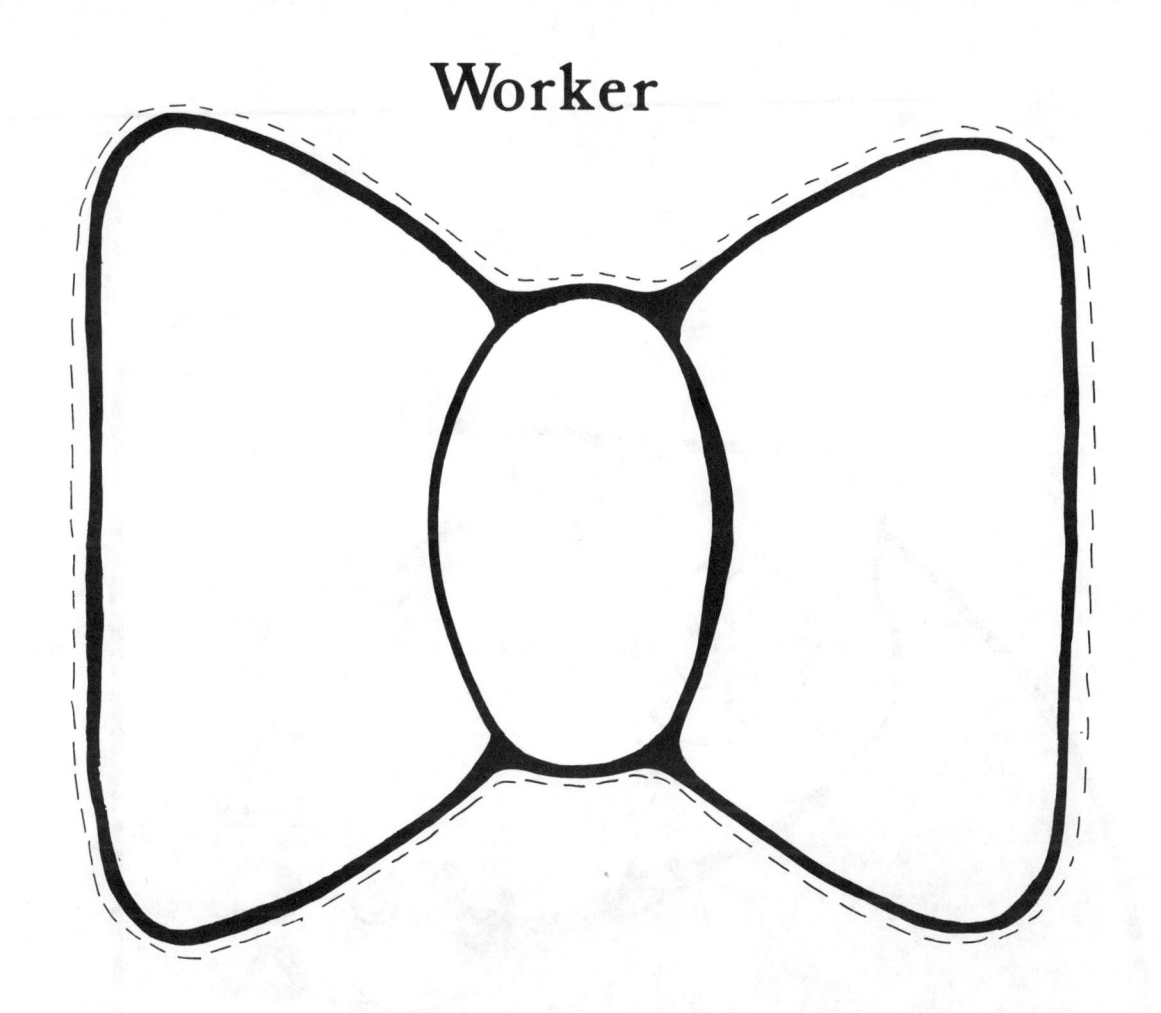

Computer Whiz

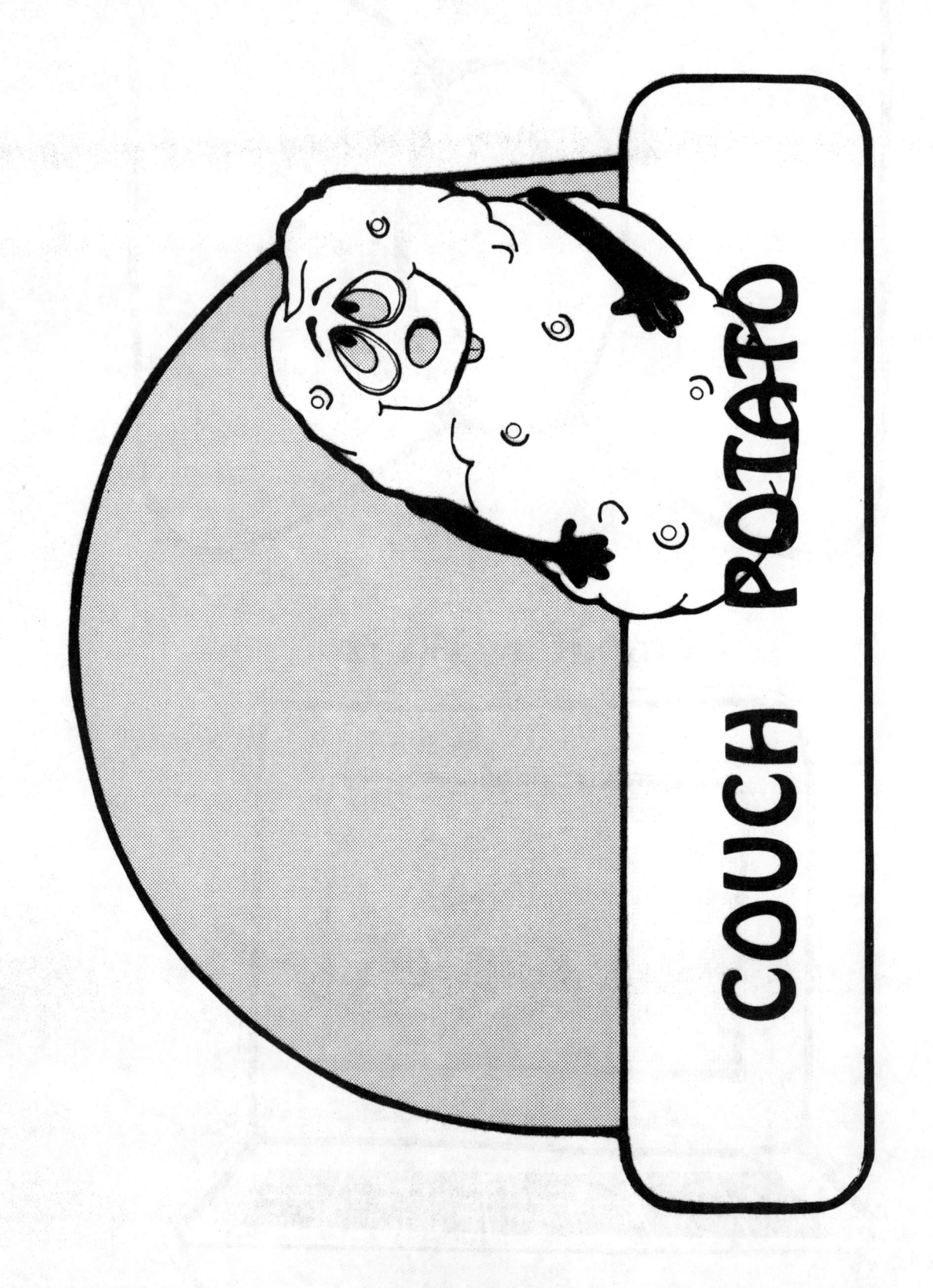

COUCH POTATO

Sailing Away

Culminate the remaining days with your class in a memorable and creative way. This Sailing Away unit can be started a week or so prior to school closing, beginning with the display of your bulletin board to establish the mood. Set aside a short time each day to read orally to students. Explore with the famous navigators or imagine with the pirates as you share thrilling literature with your class. Use a large map to demonstrate the scope of these early explorations. Talk about the risks involved in these adventures, and relate to the children that they, too, in their lives will be confronted with making decisions and taking risks. Spin a few yarns about adventures that you/they have had and how we can learn and grow from these experiences. Incorporate information about their new class or new school they will be attending next year, so that their fears can be put into perspective. Encourage older siblings, guidance counselors, and teachers from upper grades/new schools to share information with your class. If possible, arrange a field trip to the new school or classroom. Perhaps spend part of the day going through scheduled classes with the new teachers. Involve all of your students in planning the "sail"ebration ceremony so that they can continue teamwork in preparation for the final journey with you as the school year closes. Take time to enjoy your children as the last memories are etched into the sand before the tide rolls out.

DIGGING UP

Titles:
Digging Up Treasures
Looking for Good Work
Digging Up Clues/Key Words/Vocabulary (any subject)
In Search of a Good Book
Dig into . . . (your choice)
Searching for . . .
I Dig . . .
A Treasury of . . .

Materials:
1. Yellow paper for background
2. Black letters
3. Large, colorful pirate
4. Coins, maps, treasure chests, etc., on which you will display what you want the bulletin board to depict

MAPMAKER

1. Get a sheet of white paper and your crayons or markers.
2. Place your paper in front of you so that it looks like this:
3. At the center top edge, write a capital N, for north. Make a capital S for south at the bottom in the center of your paper.
4. Along the right side of your paper in the middle, place a capital E for east. Directly across on the left side write W for west.
5. In the NE part of your paper draw the front half of a ship sailing into your picture. Put a few sails on it.
6. Write the initials of your best friend on one sail.
7. Draw a flag on your ship.
8. In the SW section of your paper draw a large pirate.
9. Add land from the W side of your paper to the SE side.
10. Draw three palm trees in the SE.
11. Around the ship and the land, add water.
12. To the left of the palm tree draw an opened treasure chest.
13. To the right of the pirate draw a shovel with some overturned dirt nearby.
14. Sketch four seashells in the S part of your paper.
15. Print your name on the ship.
16. Draw a hat on your pirate. Color it black.
17. In the NW corner of your paper draw three birds.
18. Add a sword to your pirate.
19. In the treasure chest draw something you would like to find in your possession.
20. Color your picture. Check to see that you have completed all of the above directions.

LET'S "SAIL"EBRATE

Decorations

A Treasure Island look or seaside setting would be the perfect decor for the end-of-school or graduation party. Place a few large palm trees or large tropical foliage plants around the room. Using cardboard, make the entrance to the room resemble a door on a ship. Display student murals, flagships they have designed during the study of the unit. Attach a cardboard ship or waves to the refreshment table. Or get several wooden barrels and place the food around the room for a cozy atmosphere. An old trunk might be used to hold the diplomas or certificates. A walkway created by knotted rope could guide the parents to wooden benches for seating. Other decorations might include seashells, fishnets, ship's wheel, fish tanks, and anything suitable your children might offer.

Refreshments

See the ideas presented or allow your students to plan a menu.

Favors

Children love to receive party favors. The pirate cup has been provided for your use, as well as the pirate's hat. You might also try soliciting at a nearby Long John Silver's or Captain D's. Sometimes they have comic books, food coupons, hats, or other goodies children love.

Entertainment

Check the suggestions given in this section. Be sure the ones you provide are suitable to the people participating.

Ceremony

Add your personal touch to the actual program or ceremony. Jazz it up with a song or two of your choice. You may or may not want to add wearing of the hats during all or part of the ceremony. A sample dialogue for the program follows on the next page. Write your agenda on the program provided.

FOOD ? DIG IN !

The refreshments for your Pirate Party can be as inexpensive and easy as you wish. If you are working with a generous budget, let your imagination do the spending for you. Keep in mind the number of guests you will be serving and the amount of time you have for preparation. Keep in mind, also, the age and likes of the students being honored.

The ideas below are merely suggestions. Please mix, match, eliminate, or add foods of your choice. Actual recipes can be obtained from your favorite cookbooks.

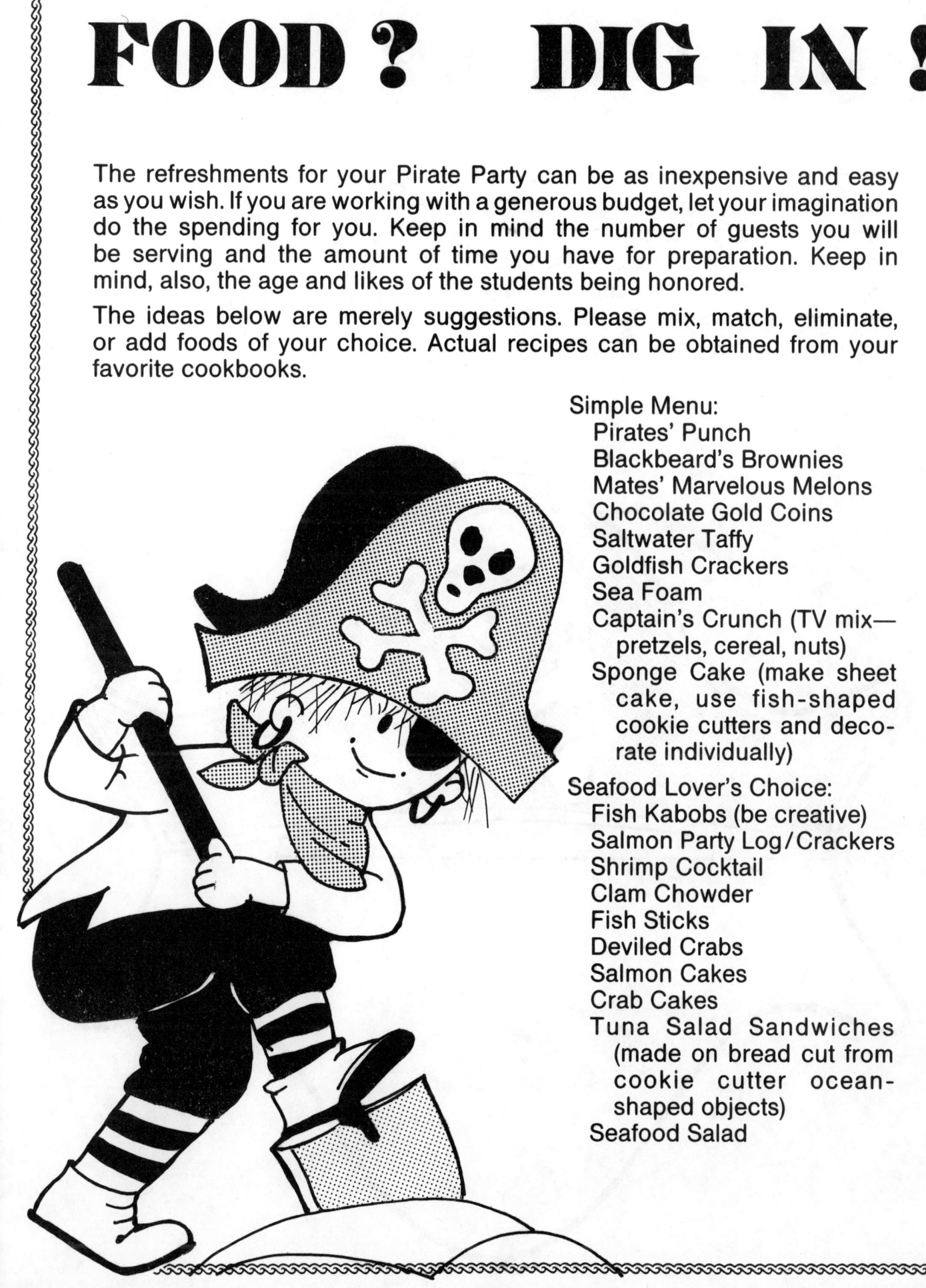

Simple Menu:
- Pirates' Punch
- Blackbeard's Brownies
- Mates' Marvelous Melons
- Chocolate Gold Coins
- Saltwater Taffy
- Goldfish Crackers
- Sea Foam
- Captain's Crunch (TV mix—pretzels, cereal, nuts)
- Sponge Cake (make sheet cake, use fish-shaped cookie cutters and decorate individually)

Seafood Lover's Choice:
- Fish Kabobs (be creative)
- Salmon Party Log/Crackers
- Shrimp Cocktail
- Clam Chowder
- Fish Sticks
- Deviled Crabs
- Salmon Cakes
- Crab Cakes
- Tuna Salad Sandwiches (made on bread cut from cookie cutter ocean-shaped objects)
- Seafood Salad

PARTY FAVOR

Delight your students with this simple favor. Make several copies of the hat before using oaktag. Color them before you cut them out. Insert a small paper cup in the center and fill it with chocolate gold coins. Saltwater taffy might be another good choice.

PIRATE HAT

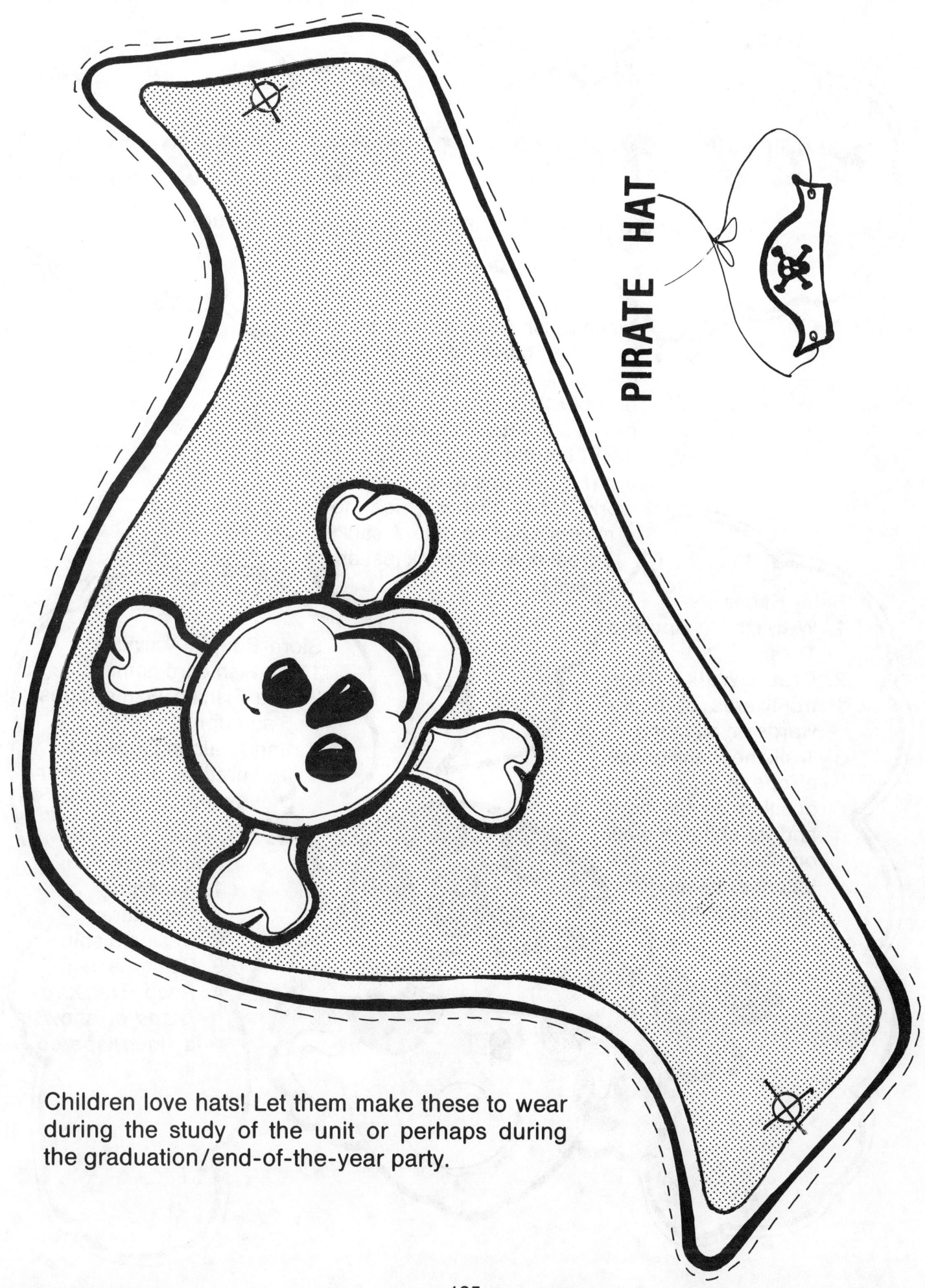

Children love hats! Let them make these to wear during the study of the unit or perhaps during the graduation/end-of-the-year party.

FUN FOR THE CREW

Involve the whole class in large or small group fun!

Make a fish pond in your classroom by blocking off a small corner. Attach a magnet to the end of a fishing pole. Buy small prizes and attach a paper clip to each. Let the children "fish" for a prize, perhaps as a reward for work done. (Fisher Price now makes a fishing pole. A stick or real pole will work just as well.)

Relay Races:
1. Wet/Dry Sponge Toss
2. Crab Walk (race frontwards or backwards on all fours)
3. Walk the Plank (place a rope in a particular position on the floor and let children walk on it or use a low balance beam for older students)

Store-Bought Activities:
1. Go Fish card game
2. The Fishing Game (ages 5 and up)
3. Sand Painting (use colored sand or buy your own)

Homemade Fun:
1. Sandbox Sculptures
2. Design a ship.
3. Design a flag.
4. Read *Treasure Island* or show a video tape of it.

PROGRAM

Welcome:

Ho, and welcome aboard! Our galleon boasts some of the finest mates this port has ever seen. We have been on this ship for a year, and during that time, we have challenged rough as well as calm seas. We have enjoyed our fellow comrades as we sailed into unknown waters. As we gather here today, may you know that our "treasure chests" are quite full and our horizon is a little bit brighter.

Class Poem: (recited by entire class or read by one student)

> Last September as we set sail
> Upon the glistening sea,
> We joined our fearless Captain—
> A younger crew were we.
> We put our thoughts together
> So we could think and dream—
> We had some sad and happy times,
> We grew to be a team.
> Our minds were just like sponges,
> Absorbing lots of "treasures";
> Our hearts became a pirate's chest
> Capturing life's pleasures.

Reminisce About the Past Year:

And now _____ (name of person) would like to spin a few yarns about our mates.

Pirates' Pledge: (recited by entire class or by fellow classmate)

After a full year of trying to do their best, may I/we share with you the Pirates' Pledge:

> I promise to keep my body healthy through proper nourishment, plenty of sleep, and physical activity;

> I promise to study the universe and those things in it to help me gain a better understanding of my world;

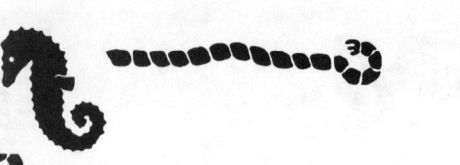

I promise to work with others as a team so that I may develop successful relationships;

I promise to stay adventuresome so that I may learn something new every day;

I promise to calculate my decisions carefully so that I may reach my destination.

Announcement: (made by someone in the audience who will bring the bottle containing the list of graduates or children involved in the ceremony to the stage)

Aye, Captain! Crew! (person comes through audience with bottle raised for all to see) Look! From the depths of the sea this bottle has washed ashore, and inside, a note! Let's see . . . (Takes note from bottle and reads: "Graduates from _____ School, 19___." Hands list to the presenter of the certificates who proceeds to read all the names.)

Presentation of Certificates:
Presentor passes out diplomas or awards.

Song or Closing Remarks:
Add your own message or song.

Finale:
Let us now partake of the plunder. (Children involved in the ceremony may now escort parents/friends to the refreshment table.)

JOLLY ROGER REVIEW

List your students graduating alphabetically. Use more than one page if necessary. Cut out the form on the dotted lines, roll it up, and insert it into a bottle. Give it to a designated student in the audience to bring up to the stage during the ceremony.

Graduates from _____ School:

1.
2.
3.
4.
5.
6.
7.
8.
9.
10.
11.
12.
13.
14.
15.
16.
17.
18.
19.
20.
21.
22.
23.
24.
25.
26.
27.
28.
29.
30.

MEDAL OF HONOR

Delight your class with this decorative medal. Make medals from oaktag or construction paper. Cut them out, write messages on them, and laminate them before giving them to students.

Try these ideas or use your own:

swiftest sailor	marvelous mate	best navigator
creative cook	smoothest sailor	log keeper
best buccaneer	black patch (honesty)	super swabby
delightful deckhand	sunniest sailor	neatest treasure chest
high seas swashbuckler	Jolly Roger attendant	pleasant pirate
creative crewman	studious sailor	first lieutenant
second lieutenant	jovial journalist	most improved crewman

SUPER SAILOR AWARD

IS PRESENTED TO _____

ON THIS _____ DAY OF _____

AT _____

FOR SAILING THE SEAS OF LEARNING AND NAVIGATING SUCCESSFULLY TO REACH FINAL DESTINATION.

_____
Captain